The Returning Tide (1850-2000)

*A History of the
Northampton Diocese
over the last 150 years*

Derek Lance

First Published in 2000
Roman Catholic Diocese of Northampton
Bishop's House
Marriott Street
Northampton
NN2 6AW

Copyright © Derek Lance 2000

ISBN 0 9538053 0 1

Printed in England by Gemini Print Ltd., Wigan, Lancs. WN4 8DT.
Tel: 01942 712480   Fax: 01942 270702

Contents

Acknowledgements iv

Foreword by Bishop Leo McCartie v

Preface vi

A Note on the Cathedral by Fr Kenneth Payne vii

Colour Illustrations xi

William's Inheritance 1

The First Hundred Years 17

Maps 51

Ten Bishops - Personalities and Policies 55

The Council Years (1950-1975) 69

Moving Out - Moving On (1976-2000) 81

Acknowledgements

❖

Grateful thanks are due to Margaret Osborne, the Northampton Diocesan Archivist. She not only made available relevant documents and photographs, but also wrote the section 'Around the Diocese 1895-1899'.

The photographs of various places and events in Milton Keynes were supplied by Fr Paul Hardy. Fr Kenneth Payne, formerly Administrator of the Cathedral, contributed the section on the Cathedral, based partly on his 'The Cathedral of Our Lady and St. Thomas, A History and Guide'.

Canon Timothy Russ is to be thanked for his valued assistance in providing a wealth of material from his research, particularly concerning the Bishops.

The pictures of the Triptych were supplied by Sr Jean Wilcox O.D.C.

We thank the Marketing Department of Cromer for the illustration used on the front cover.

The pictures of the Dominicans on page 47 were supplied by *Gracewing Publishing*, Herefordshire.

The pictures of Norwich Cathedral were supplied by Norwich Cathedral publicity officer and are printed with permission.

Foreword

❖

On 29 September 1850, the English Hierarchy was restored and the Diocese of Northampton was established with Bishop William Wareing, Vicar Apostolic of the Eastern District, as its first bishop.

This book gives a brief history of the Diocese over the last one hundred and fifty years and I take this opportunity of thanking Father Derek Lance for all the painstaking care he has given to its writing. In his task, he has been greatly helped by Canon Timothy Russ, Father Kenneth Payne and Mrs Margaret Osborne, the diocesan archivist. They, too, deserve our grateful thanks.

Many have been the changes over the last one hundred and fifty years. Perhaps the most significant was the division of the diocese in 1976 and the establishment of the Diocese of East Anglia. The Auxiliary Bishop of Northampton, Bishop Alan Clark, became the first Bishop of East Anglia which embraced the counties of Cambridge, Norfolk and Suffolk and, incidentally, as I am often reminded, all those lovely seaside parishes!

This history records the immense growth of the Catholic population over the last one hundred and fifty years and the way in which the pastoral care of the people has developed.

There have also been significant changes in relationships. Perhaps the most striking is the relationship between our Church and the other Christian communities. Gone now is that hostility which was so common in 1850 and there is in place a firm commitment to the pilgrimage towards Christian Unity.

And our relationship with our country has changed. We have become a mainstream Church with an accepted rôle in the voice and in the civic life of our country and with this change there have come expectations.

A book of memories! But memories are not just about the past, they can encourage us and enlighten us as we face the challenges of the New Millennium.

May this record be for us a source of pride in the past and an encouragement for the future.

❖ Leo McCartie

Bishop of Northampton

Preface

❖

THE RETURNING TIDE

For the Diocese of Northampton, as restored in 1850, the sea was a reality. It was the sea that formed the Eastern boundary along the Norfolk and Suffolk coast.

But, for Matthew Arnold, in his poem 'Dover Beach', the sea was also an image of faith - The Sea of Faith. He speaks of the decline of faith as the ebbing of the tide - The Sea of Faith's 'melancholy, long, withdrawing roar'.

The Catholic Church in England, suffering persecution and repression for three hundred years, had experienced that ebbing tide, even if isolated, little pools remained.

The history of Northampton Diocese, over the past century and a half, is the story of the returning tide of that Sea of Faith.

Derek Lance

The Cathedral of Our Lady and Saint Thomas

❖

In the nineteenth century the Catholic Church in this country began to revive after nearly three hundred years of persecution and suppression. Building churches and schools to cater for the increased numbers of Catholics and their needs became imperative.

Thus it was that in 1821 a Catholic priest was installed for a few months in a house in Abington Street in Northampton. Two years later, Fr William Foley, who was at the time supplying at Cresswell in Staffordshire, although his more permanent base was at the Seminary at Oscott, was about to set off on holiday to the East Coast. Bishop Milner, who was in charge of the Midland District of the country, which at that time included Northamptonshire, Norfolk and Suffolk, asked him to establish contact with some of the known Catholics in the places through which he was to pass.

The Catholics were few and far between, but as a result of Fr Foley's investigations, Dr Milner decided to establish a regular mission in Northampton itself and to send Fr Foley to start it off. He would be able to look after not only the small group of Catholics in the area, but also the considerable group of Irish soldiers stationed both in the barracks in Northampton and also at Weedon.

Fr Foley arrived in Northampton in November 1823 and managed to rent a small house on Black Lion Hill, using one room as a chapel. By the following year, his enthusiasm and untiring efforts bore fruit and he had enough money to purchase land at a quiet spot in the country, as it then was, on the Kingsthorpe Road. It was, in fact, part of the land which, in an earlier century, had been in the possession of St. Andrew's Priory, the same from which Thomas Becket had escaped. The reason for the choice of a quiet spot out of town was probably governed by the price Fr Foley could afford. He was a man with somewhat grandiose ideas, as Fr Gerard Collins writes in his notes on Foley:

'Originally Fr Foley had in mind to build a school for boys which he hoped would become a preparatory school for St. Mary's Oscott. He thought it might perhaps be called 'Little St. Mary's'. He wanted a staff of several priests. Fr Husenbeth and Fr Morgan were sounded about the possibility of joining the staff. There was to be a community of priests who at weekends would go out into the country to various Mass centres that would be started up, just as they did at Oscott. He thought he would have a farm at Northampton which would produce food for the house. He would need recreational space. With all these schemes in mind, he considered a place out in the country, not in the town. In the end he had to settle for two acres on the edge of the town, but even this was larger than would normally have been necessary for a Catholic Chapel of these times.

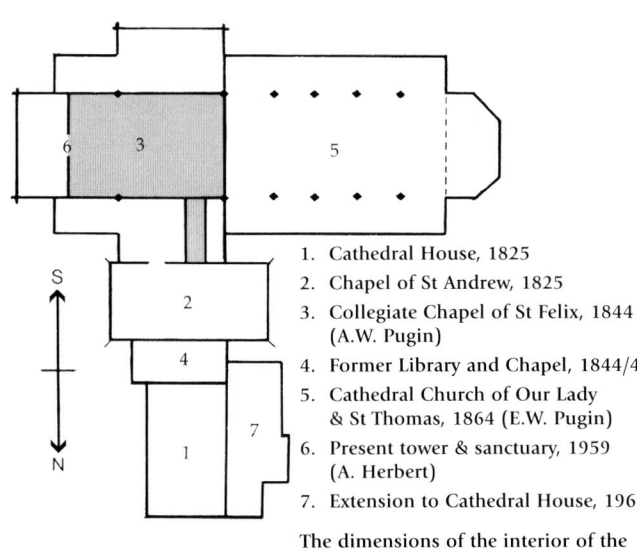

1. Cathedral House, 1825
2. Chapel of St Andrew, 1825
3. Collegiate Chapel of St Felix, 1844 (A.W. Pugin)
4. Former Library and Chapel, 1844/45
5. Cathedral Church of Our Lady & St Thomas, 1864 (E.W. Pugin)
6. Present tower & sanctuary, 1959 (A. Herbert)
7. Extension to Cathedral House, 1968

The dimensions of the interior of the present Cathedral are: Length: 160 feet
Height of tower: 95 feet
Width at transepts: 70 feet

He had to persuade Bishop Milner and Fr Walsh, the Vicar General, later Bishop Coadjutor and later still Bishop of the District, of his schemes. Although he was in correspondence with Fr Morgan and Fr Husenbeth, as well as the Bishop, they kept the whole scheme carefully under wraps, partially for fear of upsetting vested interests. When, therefore, building began there was speculation amongst the clergy about the size of the establishment. In reply to a question about the size, Fr Foley replied, *"Who knows what Providence intends".'*

The bulk of the money for the project came not from various appeals that were made, but from Fr George Morgan, who was a well-off young man from the West Country and whom Fr Foley had known at Oscott. However, despite Fr Foley's hopes, George Morgan did not join him on his 'staff' and Fr Foley never had the clerical companions he had hoped for.

The chapel, which we assume was dedicated to St. Andrew, as this is how Fr Foley headed his letters at that time, was opened on 25 October 1825. St. Andrew was a most appropriate dedication, of course, after the Priory which had stood nearby. The opening was on the feast of St. Crispin, although Fr Foley did not seem to have been aware of this until it was humorously pointed out to him - St. Crispin being the patron of leather workers. A volunteer choir of local Protestants sang the Mass and apparently the chapel was mostly filled with Protestants, the congregation of Catholics having stayed away purposely in order to accommodate them. It appears that Fr Foley was constantly receiving converts into the Church, in addition to looking after his growing mission and the small school he had set up in the house.

Northampton Cathedral undergoing construction work, October 1956

In 1829, he had ten pupils, two of whom were Francis and William Amherst, the former destined to be Bishop in Northampton 29 years later and, only a few months after the completion of the buildings, some 80 Catholics were attending Mass. Fr Foley, after celebrating the first Sunday Mass, would ride on horseback to Weedon to say Mass for the soldiers and then back to Norhampton for a third Mass at the end of the morning, all this having fasted from midnight, according to the discipline of the Church at that time.

Thus were laid not only the foundations of some of the buildings still in use today, but more importantly, through Fr Foley's pastoral zeal, enthusiasm and care for people, were laid the foundations of a good and faithful Catholic community of today.

By 1840, many more local people were using the small chapel of St. Andrew. Clearly more space was needed and so Bishop Wareing, who had been appointed in charge of the newly created Eastern District, took up residence in the house and commissioned the building of a Collegiate Chapel to be dedicated to St. Felix, Saint of East Anglia. It was designed by Augustus Welby Pugin and built adjacent to the earlier chapel. The latter was converted into dormitory accommodation for the Seminary students who, in 1845, were transferred from their Seminary in Gifford Hall, Suffolk, to Northampton. The small space between what is now Cathedral House and the original chapel of St. Andrew was 'filled in' with a library on the ground floor and a private chapel for the Bishop on the first floor. The former is now, since 1986, the Cathedral bookshop and the latter, since the reordering of the house in 1968, is the Administrator's quarters.

Cathedral

Bishop's House, Northampton

The story, in a sense, repeats itself for, with ever increasing numbers of Catholics, the Collegiate Chapel was itself soon overflowing on a Sunday and so the new Bishop Amherst asked Pugin's son, Edward Welby Pugin, to extend it to become a Cathedral. The hierarchy had, of course, been restored by this time and the Diocese of Northampton had been created. The extension, the present nave, was opened in 1864, having been joined on to the then existing Collegiate Chapel. The altar was positioned at the West End and the dedication changed to Our Lady and St. Thomas of Canterbury. Once again, stone from the surrounding terrain was used and the builder employed was the same that built the present Guildhall in the town centre. In fact, the foundation stones were laid in the same year.

Soon, in 1877, the Bishop was to move out of Cathedral House to another house in Semilong until such time as he was able to occupy the house donated by Mrs Lyne Stephens, situated behind the Cathedral in Marriott Street.

For the following ninety years, there was little change in the Cathedral. However, in 1955, Bishop Leo Parker felt that there should be a more fitting building to warrant the name 'Cathedral'. Thus it was that the 1844 Collegiate Chapel was demolished to make way for a far more spacious West End joined, of course, to the Pugin nave and with the altar once again at the East End. Further minor modifications were made in 1976 when an altar was placed in the crossing, beneath the tower, in order to make it easier to carry out the liturgical reforms of the Second Vatican Council. The whole complex was set off with a pleasing aspect from the road by the construction of the piazza-cum-car park in 1988.

In 1998, a general refurbishing of the Cathedral took place and this involved levelling part of the sanctuary to accommodate chairs for concelebrating clergy grouped around the Bishop's throne; new lighting;

Bishop Riddell's account of how Bishop's House was paid for.

The Sanctuary in 1976

The reordered Sanctuary 1999

devotional shrines to Our Lady and St. Thomas in the South Transept; the font re-sited in the North Transept; and a Triptych by Stephen Foster on the East wall depicting the Holy Spirit renewing the face of the earth. In the context of the Great Jubilee of 2000, this Triptych expresses a vision of the Holy Spirit with a new outpouring of grace which renews and redeems.

At the top of the centre panel, the Holy Spirit descends from the glory of heaven, radiating beams of light, which flow in streams, enlightening all creation. From the central cross that unites all things, flow the waters of sacramental life, flowing down, bringing new life and rebirth to creation. *(Ezechiel 47:1-12)*

In the middle, amidst the arid desert of the world, we see humanity reaching up, yearning for the gift of Pentecost, echoing the words of the Psalms, 'Like a dry weary land ...' And again, 'Like a deer that yearns for running streams.'

The two side panels are the two great doorways through which God's people enter into the vision.

On one we see the Church, infused with the Holy Spirit, proclaiming the Word of God to her children. With the light of grace He enlightens us and leads us into eternal life. *(John 16:5-15)* On the other, the manifestation of God is expressed in the Eucharist, the Spirit of love through which the Bread of Heaven transforms and unites our hearts. *(John 6:56-59)*

(Rev Kenneth Payne)

The Returning Tide - Northampton Diocese 1850-2000

The Triptych

The Triptych - carved wood by Stephen Foster

Side panel Proclaiming the Word

Side panel The Gift of the Eucharist

The Returning Tide - Northampton Diocese 1850-2000

Northampton Cathedral

The Sanctuary, before reordering

The Sanctuary, after reordering

Northampton Cathedral

Bishop's House, Northampton

*Bishop Wareing
(1850-1858)*

*Bishop Amherst
(1858-1879)*

*Bishop Riddell
(1880-1907)*

*Bishop Keating
(1908-1921)*

The Returning Tide - Northampton Diocese 1850-2000

*Bishop Carey-Elwes
(1921-1932)*

*Bishop Youens
(1933-1939)*

*Bishop Parker
(1941-1967)*

*Bishop Grant
(1967-1982)*

The Returning Tide - Northampton Diocese 1850-2000

*Bishop Thomas
(1982-1988)*

*Bishop McCartie
(1990-present)*

1.
William's Inheritance
❖

In the Autumn of 1850, William Wareing entered into his inheritance. He became the Bishop of the newly named Diocese of Northampton.

Certainly, in this context, the name Northampton was new, but that was all. It is not as if the fact of a Catholic Bishop, or Diocese for this Eastern part of England was an innovation. The Catholic Hierarchy in England was restored in 1850, not inaugurated.

Bishop William Wareing

William Wareing, a Bishop of the Catholic Church, was in a long line of succession stretching back for almost two millennia. As Bishop, he was a successor of the Apostles and the territory of Northampton Diocese had been ruled and cared for by Bishops in that same Apostolic succession for centuries. Perhaps his situation might usefully be likened to that of the most recent heir of some ancient landed family who now enters into his inheritance of the family estates, from which the family had been exiled for a period. Now he can return and take up his rightful place.

Presumably, one of the first things such an heir would do would be to look over the estate, its lands and buildings and accounts, to see what his inheritance amounted to. When Bishop William entered into his inheritance in the Diocese, he did the same and he found it to be what might best be described as impoverished.

His Diocese covered seven counties - Buckinghamshire, Bedfordshire, Northamptonshire, Huntingdonshire, Cambridgeshire, Norfolk and Suffolk - an area of some 7000 square miles, stretching from the Thames opposite Windsor to the Wash. It was, at that time, the largest Diocese in England. There were few towns of any size and most of the territory was rural, stretching from the wooded Chilterns in the South, through the agricultural lands in Northamptonshire and East Anglia to the expanses of the Fens beyond Cambridge and the remote areas of heath and woodland around Norwich and on to the long coastline that formed its Eastern border. Agriculture and fishing would be the main occupations. The earlier, prosperous wool trade had by now declined and the new industries were concentrated not here, but in the North and Midlands. Even the large country houses and landed estates, such as Harrowden near Northampton, or Sawston near Cambridge, had known better times, especially if the families had been recusant Catholics and thus subject to the onerous fines of Penal times.

Sawston Hall

Although some main lines had been built, the railway system was still in its infancy and not much in evidence in these Eastern counties. The horse or carriage remained the usual means of transport. And although the Penny Post had been introduced in 1840, communications throughout this vast Diocese were still extremely difficult. Not only was Northampton the largest Diocese, but it lacked a natural centre. The town of Northampton was a rather awkward and unwieldy position for a centre. Later, in 1890, the Canons suggested to the then Bishop Riddell that he might move to Cambridge, making the newly built grand church there his Cathedral, but this was rejected. Looking back on this early period, Bishop Parker, in 1952, wrote, 'Wales and the Eastern projection of England seem, as it were, to have been portions of Great Britain which were left over when the country was divided up into Dioceses at the time of the revival of the Hierarchy of Ecclesia Anglicana in 1850. The other Dioceses had some centre of unity - London, Liverpool, Birmingham, but not Northampton'. He notes that even in the nineteen-fifties it was difficult to hold meetings or conferences and so he promoted the Diocesan magazine as a way of alleviating the difficulty of maintaining contact. How much greater was that difficulty for Bishop Wareing.

Nevertheless, Bishop Wareing did make contact and was able to give an account of the Catholic life of the Diocese in his report to Rome in 1854. After again pointing out that his is the largest Diocese in England, he says that he has no 'palace' and no Cathedral, but has good hopes of constructing part of a larger and more beautiful church which in course of time may grow into a Cathedral. The small church of St. Felix, he describes as a 'pro-Cathedral'. Religious services, owing to the rural nature of the Diocese, cannot be properly carried out. The Blessed Sacrament is not always kept in church, but in the presbytery for fear of profanation and sacrilege. The Catholic population he estimates at 10,000, of whom 1,000 are at Norwich, 600 at Northampton and others in scattered places. Whilst there are Jesuits at Norwich, Bury St. Edmunds and Yarmouth and one Benedictine at Bungay, priests (presumably 'seculars') number 30 - 'all natives'. In 1850, there had been 27 priests and 26 parishes or Mass centres. There is one convent. Among the evils of the Diocese, he refers to mixed marriages, neglect of Feasts, consort with non-Catholics due to this heresy-infected area, poverty and fewness of Catholics. No schools are mentioned. When Bishop Amherst succeeded Wareing in 1858, he could still describe the Diocese as ' in a most destitute condition, fifty years behind the rest of England... in want of priests and money'. Even so, it seems rather extreme for Cardinal Manning to have referred to the Diocese as 'the dead See'.

This state of the Diocese would not have come as a surprise to Bishop Wareing, because he had moved to Northampton in 1840 when, as Titular Bishop of Aristopolis, he had been Vicar Apostolic of the Eastern District, which is the area that became the Northampton Diocese. For ten years he had, in effect, been Bishop of Northampton in all but name. Nor would Bishop Wareing have been entirely without hope as he began his episcopate, because by 1850 the situation for Catholics in England had been improving somewhat since the beginning of the century.

The twenty years between 1780 and 1800 witnessed the lowest point ever reached by the Catholic Church in England since, perhaps, the tenth century. The long years of persecution and suppression had taken their toll. By 1800, there was but a single priest in each of the counties of Bedford, Buckingham, Cambridge and Northampton and only an exiled Frenchman in Huntingdon.

Priest in late 18th century

Signs of Hope

Then the tide had begun to turn. Slowly things improved. In 1791, the building of public chapels was legalised and the Catholic Emancipation Act of 1829 removed many of the civil disabilities under which Catholics had suffered for so long. The number of Catholics in England had been steadily increasing. This was, perhaps, most notable in the industrial North and Midlands where there was a growing number of Catholic operatives and unskilled labourers in the mills and collieries and working as navvies on the building of the railways and canals.

Many of these were immigrants from Ireland who had come to England in large numbers after the development of regular steam navigation between the two countries which had begun in 1825, and even before the Irish famine augmented their numbers. There was, also, a growing class of Catholic businessmen and manufacturers in places like Liverpool, Newcastle, Manchester and Birmingham, some of whom were connected by marriage to the old Catholic gentry. The colleges of Ushaw, Oscott, Sedgley Park and Old Hall were beginning to expand rapidly. In London there was developing a similar class, to which the Wiseman family belonged, of manufacturers and merchants as well as Catholic lawyers. All this, however, was concentrated in the North and Midlands or London, with little to show in the Eastern District. But there was also the British army which, since the Peninsular war, contained many thousands of Catholic soldiers, mostly of Irish origin. It was the concentration of Catholic soldiers at Weedon in Northamptonshire that prompted the setting up of a mission there, one of the earliest in the area of Northampton Diocese.

Cardinal John Henry Newman

A further contribution to this slowly recovering Catholic Church in England came from the Oxford Movement in the Anglican Church and the subsequent conversions. The most notable of these was, of course, John Henry Newman who became a Catholic in 1845, but there were others who were connected with the Northampton Diocese either by birth or by association. George Spencer, for instance, the youngest son of Earl Spencer of Althorp had become the Church of England Vicar of Great Brington, just on the edge of the Althorp estate. While visiting some soldiers in the Northampton barracks, he met Fr Foley of Northampton. They became friends and, in 1830, George Spencer was received into the Catholic Church by Fr Caestryck O.P. in Leicester. He was ordained a priest and served in the Midland District. Then, inspired by Fr Dominic Barberi C.P., who had received Newman, Fr George Spencer, too, joined the Passionist Order as Fr Ignatius and devoted himself to the cause of Christian unity, leading a crusade of prayer for the removal of prejudice and the promotion of charity and mutual co-operation.

A little later, Frederick Faber, who was the Church of England Vicar at Elton, also near Northampton, came with many of his parishioners to be received into the Catholic Church by Bishop Wareing in the Collegiate Chapel in Northampton in 1844. He, too, went on to be ordained a priest. He is, of course, the famous Fr Faber who, with Newman, joined the Congregation of the Oratory and, while Newman founded the Oratory in Birmingham, Fr Faber set one up in London, the well known Brompton Oratory. Other converts to Rome, influenced by the Oxford Movement, who had connections with Northampton Diocese, were de Lisle, Fr Morris and Canon Bernard Smith.

Recollections

Bishop William Wareing

We can picture Bishop Wareing sitting in his little house in Northampton, surveying his Diocese and composing his report for Rome. While he enumerates the difficulties and paucity of resources, it is also possible that recollection of these signs of recovery, these early shoots of Newman's 'Second Spring', will have encouraged him to hope. But it is also possible, even likely, that his mind may have gone back to earlier times. He may have recalled, perhaps rather wistfully, how the faith first came to this area and how, over the centuries, the Church here had grown and flourished. All this, too, was his inheritance and it is ours which we, too, need to recall and have as our inspiration.

The Returning Tide - Northampton Diocese 1850-2000

Beginnings

Certainly the Catholic faith first came to Britain in Roman times and the first recorded martyr, St. Alban, suffered probably in 209. Then, in 597, St. Augustine and his monks came to convert the pagan Angles, Saxons and Jutes who had occupied Britain after the Romans had departed, but this mission was confined largely to Kent and Essex.

The area of what was to become the Diocese of Northampton received the faith somewhat later. The Eastern part - East Anglia (Norfolk, Suffolk, Cambridgeshire) - owes its conversion principally to St. Felix, a monk from Burgundy, who became the first Bishop of Dunwich and who died in 646, and to St. Edmund, king of East Anglia, who was martyred in 870.

As for the more Western area, we look to St. Birinius who came as a missionary and established his Episcopal See at Dorchester-on-Thames in 636. It was, perhaps, missionaries from the Isle of Lindisfarne who had the greatest impact on the Middle Angles of our region. We must especially note St. Chad who established his See at Lichfield, which included the region of our present Northampton Diocese. After the Episcopal See had been transferred to different places a few times, so that our area was under a variety of Diocesan names, finally in 1072, Remigius, the last Bishop of Dorchester-on-Thames, was translated to Lincoln. The area of our present Northampton Diocese remained under the jurisdiction of Lincoln for many centuries.

During that time, up to the sixteenth century, the Church in our region continued to grow and, indeed, to flourish. The Catholic life then was so rich and all-pervasive, affecting every part of society, that it is not possible to give a detailed, systematic history of it here. Instead, we may appreciate and get a flavour of our heritage by recalling a few images, or snapshots.

Abbeys and Cathedrals

In the post-Norman Conquest landscape, in addition to the growing number of parish churches and castles, a prominent feature was the several monastic abbeys and priories. In our region these were chiefly Benedictine. When St. Benedict had formed his first monasteries and given them 'The Rule' in the sixth century, he had in mind a relatively small community living away from the towns and being self-sufficient. Over time, and certainly by the eleventh century, the monasteries in Europe and England had become much larger and often towns had grown up around them. Although still living by the same Rule, they were now very much involved in the local feudal community and especially in farming. They not only had more extensive buildings, but often farmed large areas in which they had manors. In the thirteenth century, for example, the abbey at Bury St. Edmunds had 170 manors. But they were still houses of prayer, centres of evangelisation and a focus for the religious life of their neighbourhood. Certainly up to the twelfth century, they were also the chief centres of learning.

Pre-Reformation Chapel of The Medieval Hospital of St. John Baptist and St. John Evangelist, Northampton

Norwich Cathedral

Norwich Cathedral cloisters

It not infrequently happened that a monk would be chosen as the Bishop and the abbey would become the Cathedral. In our region this was the case, for example, at Norwich, Peterborough, Bury St. Edmund's and Ely. Their fine churches and cloisters can still be seen today, although the Cathedrals have since been taken over by the Anglican Church. This is what Bishop Wareing would have seen as he travelled through his Northampton Diocese. Those Cathedrals at his time would have resembled not what they had been in the Middle Ages, but would be more like the picture given in the Barchester novels.

Thomas Becket

St. Thomas Becket

The first in importance of all the Cathedrals was, of course, Canterbury with its Archbishop, and it is Archbishop Thomas Becket who has a very special relationship with Northampton Diocese. He was taken as patron of the Diocese.

Thomas at first held a post in the household of Theobald, the Archbishop of Canterbury, who ordained him Deacon and subsequently Archdeacon. Employed on many important assignments, Thomas came to the notice of King Henry II with whom he became a close friend. In 1154, the King appointed Thomas Chancellor and, as such, Thomas had a magnificent court. When Theobald died, the King appointed Thomas as his successor and so Thomas was ordained priest on 2 June 1162 and Archbishop of Canterbury on the following day.

Thomas then adopted a more austere, ascetical manner of life and showed that he was totally dedicated to serving God. Thomas' uncompromising stand on certain principles brought him into conflict with King Henry. At first it was a difference over relatively minor matters, but then it became more serious. There followed a series of clashes over the rival claims of the King's authority opposed by what Thomas saw as God's authority. Henry was baffled and infuriated by this apparently new zeal of his erstwhile friend and he now saw Thomas as a threat and an enemy. As he put it, *'England is not a bush that can hold two such robins as the Archbishop and myself'*.

The growing antagonism between the two came to a head when, in 1164, Thomas was summoned before the King and his court at the Council of Northampton, at Northampton Castle, where he defiantly challenged the King. Thomas made it clear that people must choose which to serve, either the King or the Church. He strode into the court bearing his Primatial Cross. He defied the King, refusing to allow the Church to be brought under the power of the State. He refused to hear judgement against himself and, threatening excommunication to any who consented to the trial, walked out through the crowd of courtiers, none of whom dared to touch him. After spending part of the night in St. Andrew's priory, he fled to the Kent coast and then into France. After six years in exile, he returned to Canterbury and within a few weeks, on 29 December 1170, he was murdered by four of the King's knights in the Cathedral. This martyrdom shocked the whole of Christendom and Thomas Becket was canonised in 1173 and his tomb at once became a centre of pilgrimage until 1538 when another King, Henry VIII, had it destroyed and had the martyr's bones scattered. But devotion to Becket lived on through the Reformation period and he was, and is, venerated anew in the Cathedral of Northampton.

Religious Orders

Although the early part of the Middle Ages has been called the Benedictine Centuries, there were other Religious Orders throughout England in this period and several of them figured prominently in the area of the Northampton Diocese.

Of particular interest are the Augustinians or Austin Friars at Clare in Suffolk, to the South of Bury St. Edmunds. William the Conqueror gave Erbury to Richard Fitzgilbert who built

Clare Priory

his castle over the Roman and Saxon ruins and called it the Honour of Clare. In 1098, Fitzgilbert brought some Benedictine monks from Bec in Normandy to the castle, but they did not stay long. In 1248, his great-grandson, Richard de Clare brought from France some Austin Friars. They set up their house there, Clare Priory. They later spread and founded houses in other parts of England and their first English novice at Clare was one William Sengham. King Edward I, whose daughter Joan had married Gilbert de Clare, visited the Priory in 1298. Joan, who had added a chapel of St. Vincent to the Priory, was later buried there in 1307 and her brother, King Edward II, came with all the peers of England to lay her to rest.

Joan's daughter Elizabeth, who had married Sir John de Burgh, Earl of Ulster, added a new Chapter House, dormitory and refectory. In the stained glass windows of these houses, the Red Hand of Ulster mingled with the arms of Clare. There is a further connection with Ireland in that Elizabeth's daughter, another Elizabeth, married Lionel Plantagenet, son of King Edward III, who took the title Duke of Clarence and became a great patron of the Austin Friars from Clare even to Dublin, where he tried to found a university under their direction. It is also claimed that Clare county in Ireland derived its name from the Suffolk Priory.

Part of the Friars' work was copying and distributing books of prayer. In 1317, William Yarmouth, Peter Pye and Thomas Crymplesham bought very fine breviaries there. The life of the Friars continued at Clare until the Reformation, when Henry VIII appointed one of his supporters, George Browne, to be Provincial of the Austin Friars. In 1538, the last Prior, John Halybud, surrendered the keys to the King's bailiffs and Richard Frende acquired 'the site, soil and churchyard of same'. The lands amounted to thirty-eight acres. Thus, another part of Bishop Wareing's inheritance had been lost. But in the nineteen-fifties the Austin Friars returned to Clare from Ireland and in the nineteen-nineties they celebrated with a conference at Clare College, Cambridge. This history of the Austin Friars mirrors what was happening on a larger scale to the whole Church in the Northampton Diocese area over these centuries.

Friars, University and Mystics

The thirteenth century was marked particularly by the Friars and the Universities and the two met in our region at Cambridge. First we may notice the Carmelite Friars. As far as the Northampton Diocese area is concerned, what is significant is their move from Chesterton to Newnham in 1249 and their attending the Schools, or Scholastic faculties, at Cambridge University. One part of Queens' College, which was added in the nineteenth century, is called Friar Court, being built on a site that was formerly occupied by the Carmelites. The Carmelites sold part of their site to the College in 1537 in anticipation of the Act of

Queens' College: The President's Lodge

Suppression (1539) by which the King closed many monasteries and religious houses and seized their lands and property. The King subsequently sold the rest of the site to Queens' College in 1544. Today we can see, now in the College's Old Library, several stained glass portraits of Carmelite Friars of the mediaeval period.

A distinguished Carmelite theologian of the fourteenth century was John Baconthorpe who took his name from the village of Baconthorpe near Sheringham in Norfolk. He took the habit of the Carmelite Order at Blakeney, a little way along the coast from Sheringham. He taught in various universities, including Cambridge, and died in London in 1346.

The most numerous Friars associated with Cambridge were the Franciscans. The first small band of Franciscans landed in England on the South coast in 1224. They then moved on in groups to various centres inland and two of them, Richard of Ingworth and Richard of Devon, came to Northampton. The Franciscans founded houses at Norwich (1226), Cambridge and King's Lynn (1230). At Cambridge their first chapel, dating from 1238, was befittingly modest, a day's work of a single carpenter. The Franciscans were prominent in the University and their School there was, by 1250, on an equality with that of Oxford.

The Dominicans had houses in our region as is evidenced, for example, by the still surviving Blackfriars Hall in Norwich. They were less prominent, however, at Cambridge University than were the Franciscans.

One of the most renowned Franciscans, but of the fourteenth century, was John Duns Scotus, the eminent theologian, 'the subtle doctor'. He was born in Scotland in 1266 and entered the Franciscans at Dumfries in 1281. But his connection with us is that he was ordained priest by Oliver Sutton, the Bishop of Lincoln, in St. Andrew's Church in Northampton in 1291. He defended the doctrine of the Immaculate Conception before it was defined and he was beatified in 1993.

It was in that same century, the fourteenth, that there lived in Norwich the mystic, Julian of Norwich, whose writings, 'Revelations of Divine Love', have been rediscovered in our day and whose spirituality is now having such a marked effect. Roughly her contemporary is another local mystic, Margery Kempe of King's Lynn.

Walsingham

Mention of King's Lynn immediately draws our attention to Walsingham, for the Red Mount Chapel at King's Lynn is one of the wayside chapels en route to Walsingham and when, in the twentieth century, devotion to Walsingham was reviving, it was at King's Lynn that a shrine was set up until such time as Walsingham itself could be restored.

The shrine and devotion at Walsingham began in 1061, when Lady Richeldis de Favarches, a young Saxon widow, received the promise from Our Lady, 'Whoever seeks help there, will not go away empty-handed'. And she believed that Our Lady had asked her to build a replica of the Holy House of Nazareth. So what Lady Richeldis built was a small Saxon house, not modelled on the houses of Palestine, nor an elaborate shrine. Soon pilgrims began to flock there from all over England and the Continent, including in their number kings, nobles, gentry and commoners. We have an account of the learned Erasmus making pilgrimage there. The pilgrims came, some seeking a cure, others to fulfil a vow or seeking an adventure. In any case, going on pilgrimage was a fairly common thing, as Chaucer noted.

Erasmus

To accommodate all this, a network of roads grew up lined with chapels and shrines. Hospices and inns became plentiful and a number of priories also offered hospitality. In time, a large Priory Church was built near the shrine and the Canons Regular of St. Augustine became the first custodians of the shrine.

King Henry VIII was a regular, generous benefactor and was the last of many kings to visit Walsingham before the Reformation. He is said to have walked barefoot from Barsham Manor to the Slipper Chapel, a journey of two miles.

14th Century Slipper Chapel: National Shrine of Our Lady of Walsingham

The Slipper Chapel, a mile away from the Shrine, is an interesting place. It was erected in 1338 and its name is thought to derive either from the fact that you there took off your shoes before completing the final mile barefoot, or from the Anglo-Saxon word 'slype', meaning something in between. It is suggested that Alan of Walsingham, who was responsible for much of the architectural magnificence of Ely Cathedral, may have been instrumental in building the Slipper Chapel as there are features common to both buildings.

Like so many other things of Bishop Wareing's inheritance, however, the Walsingham Shrine, its pilgrims and devotion were stopped by the Reformation. Henry VIII, formerly a pilgrim, now ordered the Shrine to be destroyed and the land confiscated. The statue of Our Lady there was taken to Chelsea and burned. The Holy House was burned to the ground and devotion was quashed for four hundred years.

Parishes and People

Walsingham was not the only shrine to which pilgrims travelled, even if it was the most renowned of our region, attracting large crowds from far afield. The veneration of Saints and going on pilgrimage to their shrines was a widespread part of the traditional religious scene that flourished right up to the eve of the Reformation, as Eamon Duffy has described in detail in his, 'The

The Mediaeval Church, Hengrave Hall

Stripping of the Altars'. His point is that there was a vigorous, healthy expression of the faith that was not confined to a particular class, or to Religious. The liturgy, celebrated in the numerous parish churches, with their pictorial representation of Christian truths, was accessible to the ordinary lay person. Far from these lay faithful being ignorant or superstitious, or their religion being in a state of corruption and decay, he has shown convincingly that they were being taught the faith well by Bishops and the Parochial Clergy. There were many vernacular religious books available and circulating among the laity, and their religion found another means of expression in the very many guilds and religious communities and associations. What is of particular interest to us is that Eamon Duffy takes most of his overwhelming accumulation of evidence for this from detailed examples of East Anglia.

Under Attack

This thriving religious life in the parishes suffered attack and attempts to destroy it by the agents of the Protestant Reformation and of the State. It suffered the same attack as did those other elements of our Catholic heritage we have noted - the Religious Orders, the Liturgy, the Catholic hierarchy, the Catholic theology and tradition. The inheritance was, in large part, destroyed, the tradition disrupted.

This attack, however, by provoking a strong resistance, created another element that would form part of the inheritance namely, the witness of the martyrs and the perseverance of a nucleus of Catholics through the sufferings of the Penal times. It was on this that the Catholic restoration in the nineteenth century was to build.

Martyrs

The earliest martyrs of this period were those who would not accept the break with Rome that followed Henry VIII's repudiation of his marriage to Catherine of Aragon and who, therefore, refused to subscribe to the Act of Supremacy and the Act of Succession which declared the King to be the Head of the Church on Earth, thus rejecting the Pope. The two most notable of these martyrs who have a connection with our region by virtue of their being members of Cambridge University, were John Houghton and John Fisher.

A Shrine of the English Martyrs, Beaconsfield

John Houghton was the Prior of the London Charterhouse, which St. Thomas More visited frequently for periods of spiritual retreat. The Carthusians there had a great reputation as spiritual directors and it was probably this that determined King Henry VIII to demand their assent to the Act of Succession. Their influence would be invaluable. They, of course, refused and suffered the penalty of martyrdom.

John Houghton, born in Essex, had come up to Cambridge University and obtained the degrees of B.A., Ll.B., and B.D. He was ordained priest at twenty-four and four years later entered the Carthusian Order at the London Charterhouse, of which he later became the Prior. When the matter of the royal supremacy arose, he warned his monks that they would soon be called upon to chose between death and renunciation of their faith and he then declared a Solemn Triduum.

Houghton was arrested, committed to the Tower of London and tried in Westminster Hall on 29 April 1535 for denying that the King was the Supreme Head of the Church on Earth. He was executed at Tyburn on 4 May 1535. After having been hanged, he was cut down and disembowelled while still living. One of his arms was hung over the gateway of the London Charterhouse.

He was not executed alone. His fellow Carthusians were also martyred along with Richard Reynolds, a member of the Brigittine Order and of Christ's College and John Haile or Hale, the Vicar of Isleworth and a Fellow of King's College, Cambridge.

John Fisher

Bishop John Fisher suffered martyrdom for the same reason seven weeks later. John Fisher, born in Beverley in 1469, went up to Cambridge at the age of fourteen and was ordained priest at twenty-two. His career at Cambridge was most distinguished. Master of Michael house (later absorbed into Trinity College) in 1497, Chancellor of the University in 1504, he was finally President of Queens' College from 1505 to 1508. He it was who was responsible for attracting Erasmus to Cambridge and Fisher himself founded lectureships and scholarships. He revived the study of Greek and Hebrew and was the first Lady Margaret Professor of Divinity. The Margaret of that title was Lady Margaret Beaufort, the mother of Henry VII. In 1502, Fisher had been appointed as her chaplain and he encouraged her to found both St. John's and Christ's Colleges.

Bishop John Fisher

In 1504, King Henry VII nominated Fisher to the Bishopric of Rochester. He earned the reputation of being a model Bishop and when offered the richer Sees of Ely and Lincoln, he declined, remaining faithful to the relatively small See of Rochester. Henry VIII boasted that no other country had so distinguished a prelate, but when Bishop Fisher opposed the King in the matter of the royal supremacy, the King turned against him. Attempts were made to kill Fisher with poisoned porridge and by a shot fired into his library and Thomas Cromwell, the King's agent, tried unsuccessfully to implicate him in treasonous plots. Finally, when Fisher refused to sign the Act of Succession, which implied that the King was the Head of the Church, displacing the Pope, he was committed to the Tower. While imprisoned there, he was made a Cardinal by Pope Paul III, which only enraged the King further. On 22 June 1535, Fisher was executed. His body was buried without a shroud or religious rites at All Hallows graveyard in Barking and his head was impaled for fourteen days on London Bridge.

The Attack Continued

The reign of Edward VI saw the advancement of Protestant doctrines and the framing of a Protestant form of worship. Then Mary Tudor attempted a Catholic restoration, but this was not successful and some of her policies alienated people further from Catholicism.

Queen Mary died in 1558 and, in the next year, two Acts of Parliament were passed which made the practice of the Catholic religion illegal, and so it remained until the Second Relief Act of 1791, a period of two-hundred and thirty-three years.

The Faith was driven underground. The loss of political rights, the denial of economic opportunity, fines, imprisonment and even death awaited those, both priest and layman, who were detected or betrayed. These were Penal times, a time of falling numbers of both Catholic laity and of priests. Whereas there had been, perhaps, 2,400,000 Catholics in England in 1559, by 1780 the number had fallen to 60,000. This decrease was all the more ominous when it is remembered that the population had risen from about 4,000,000 to some 7,500,000 in the same period. Initially the Catholics were served by the remnant of Marian priests, which never amounted to more than 2,000 and which was reduced by the end of Elizabeth's reign, through death and apostasy, to vanishing point.

Reaction and Resistance

All would have been lost had it not been for reinforcements. This started with a trickle of Dominicans in 1569. It was then powerfully strengthened and surpassed by secular clergy - the Seminary priests - from 1574, then by Jesuits from 1580 and Benedictines from 1600. By

1630 there were some 600 priests in England and Wales. But the priests were totally dependent on the laity. There were no public churches. Mass was a secret affair in some inconspicuous room, often in a country house of a Catholic family. So it was a time of a secret, hidden Church and a time of martyrs.

Martyrs

Of the very many martyrs of England and Wales of this period, a representative forty have been canonised recently in our own day. Of these, five were born in our Diocese.

Robert Southwell S.J. was born of wealthy parents at Horsham St. Faiths, just outside Norwich in 1561. Although his father conformed by going to the services of the parish church, Robert was brought up a Catholic and escaped abroad at fifteen for the sake of his education and then, after walking to Rome, was admitted to the Society of Jesus. He was a key man in the education of the students in the English College in Rome, but he returned to England in 1586. There he laboured for six years, mainly around London, purposely refraining from visiting Norfolk for fear of embarrassing his family. He spent these years as a hunted priest, encouraging others by his writings and living a life of adventure and hair's breadth escapes.

He gained a great reputation as a poet of the English literary Renaissance and was a friend and an influence on Shakespeare, and his poetry shows a deep patriotism. Hearing his father was ill, he wrote a ten page letter bidding him to think of the danger to his soul of denying his faith and begging him to seek absolution. His father did repent and died a Catholic.

Taken at last, through the treachery of one he had helped, he was tortured repeatedly by Topcliffe, but nothing could shake his fortitude. On the scaffold he said, ' I beg God that my death may be for my own and my country's good and the comfort of the Catholics, my brethren.' He was martyred at Tyburn on 21 February 1595.

Edmund Campion, a Jesuit martyr

Henry Walpole S.J. was born at Dorking in Norfolk in 1558, the cousin of the family that gave a Prime Minister to England. He was educated at Norwich Grammar School, at Peterhouse, Cambridge and, in law, at Gray's Inn. The example of Edmund Campion's heroic death brought Walpole to the Faith and in 1582 he went to Rheims and to Rome to study and to join the Society of Jesus. He was ordained priest in 1588. After a varied career including some years teaching in Spain and Flanders and a year as prisoner of the Calvinists in Holland, he returned to England. He was arrested within twenty-four hours of landing in Yorkshire. He was tortured fourteen times by Topcliffe in London. Although he seems to have been for brief periods so confused that he signed documents that subtly compromised the Faith, on regaining his senses he denounced all admissions - and they were never substantial. He was sent back to York, condemned for his priesthood and suffered a martyr's death on 7 April 1595.

John Paine was martyred somewhat earlier in 1582. Born in Northamptonshire, John Paine was ordained priest at Douai and returned to England with Cuthbert Mayne. His mission field was Essex where, disguised as steward to Lady Petre, he made Ingatestone his headquarters. The notorious Eliot betrayed him. He refused a pardon offered on condition he conformed to the new Protestant Church and was martyred at Chelmsford on 2 April 1582.

Two priests from Suffolk were martyred in the sixteen-forties.

Alban Roe was born in Suffolk in 1583. While he was a student at Cambridge, he became a Catholic, thanks to a conversation with a working man imprisoned for his faith in St.

Albans gaol, where Alban himself as a priest was later committed.

After Cambridge, he studied at Douai and Lorraine, where he joined the English Benedictines of Dieuward. In England he was in and out of gaol, including in Maiden Lane in London. He was betrayed by a lapsed Catholic and, at the beginning of the Long Parliament, was committed to Newgate for doing the work of a priest and condemned. On the scaffold, when there was no handkerchief to cover his face, he said, 'But I dare look death in the face.' The first fruit of his death was his reconciliation to God of a criminal undergoing the same sentence. Alban was martyred at Tyburn on 21 January 1642.

Henry Morse S.J. also came from Suffolk. He was born in the village of Broome in 1595, the same year in which Robert Southwell had died. He was a student at Emmanuel College, Cambridge and a law student at Gray's Inn, where he became a Catholic. He then studied at Douai and Rome, but under the pseudonym of Claxton, became a Jesuit and was ordained priest in Rome in 1625. He had a chequered career, being twice banished from England and then a third time, to save his friend, he went into voluntary exile. He was in prison in Durham, Newcastle, York and London. Abroad, he helped the English soldiers.

Back in England, his great work was ministering to the victims of the plague. He became a byword for bravery and gentleness and received about a hundred families into the Church. He caught the plague, but recovered, it was said miraculously, and began again to attend to the plague-stricken. He worked quite openly as a priest and was tolerated by his persecutors as long as the danger of the plague persisted and he was of use to them. When the plague was over, however, he was promptly arrested and condemned to death. By the intercession of the Catholic Queen, the sentence was commuted to banishment. He shortly returned to England and worked for eighteen months in Cumberland, but was then again captured and sentenced on the same charge that he 'seduced His Majesty's subjects from the religion by law established' during the plague. He was executed at Tyburn on 1 February 1645 and after his death many miracles were worked through his relics.

There were many more martyrs in this period who were connected with Northampton Diocese region either by birth, or by their mission work here. They are too numerous to be detailed here, but we may note some who were laymen.

Bryan Lacy of Hoxne in Suffolk accompanied his cousin, Fr Mountford Scott, and helped him in his missionary work in East Anglia. He is known to have been doing so, for example, in Colney, Norwich in 1583. Bryan Lacy was arrested with Fr Scott and executed at Tyburn in 1591.

Thomas Tunstall came from North Yorkshire, but worked for the Faith in Norfolk and was executed in Norwich in 1616. He spent five years in Wisbech prison, from which he escaped by dropping down a long rope and then went to Lynn. The woman who took him in and tended to his injured hands was so impressed by him that unfortunately she told her husband, who was a Justice of the Peace, all about him. He thereupon arrested Tunstall and imprisoned him at Norwich. Condemned on the evidence of a lying witness, Tunstall asked to become a Benedictine before he died and asked that his head should be put on St. Benet's gate. His wish was fulfilled. He is the only martyr to have been executed at Norwich, although many laymen were imprisoned in the Norwich Castle.

Another group of martyrs who deserve mention, and are sometimes insufficiently noticed, are the Secular, or Seminary priests. There are several of these with local connections, but the following three may suffice as examples of that group.

Everard Hanse is said to have been born in Northamptonshire. After studying at

Cambridge University, he was ordained a Protestant minister and received a benefice. After holding this for two or three years, he fell dangerously ill and, realising his perilous state, he had a discussion with a priest, who is said to have been his brother, William Hanse of Douai College. Everard was reconciled to the Catholic Church as a result and, resigning his benefice, he went to the Seminary in Rheims and was ordained a priest on 25 March 1581.

He asked to be sent on the English mission immediately and for a time stayed in London. One day, while visiting some Catholics in the Marshalsea prison, he aroused the suspicion of a gaoler that he was a priest and was arrested. On being examined, he boldly admitted that he was a Catholic priest from Rheims and was imprisoned at Newgate. After a further examination, in which Fr Hanse said that he had come to England to gain souls and that he unhesitatingly acknowledged the spiritual supremacy of the Pope, he was condemned to death. On 31 July 1581, he was martyred at Tyburn by being hanged, drawn and quartered.

Richard Newport was also from Northamptonshire, being born in 1572, possibly at Ashby St. Legers. Having been brought up a Protestant, he was converted to the Catholic Church and decided to become a priest after witnessing the execution of a priest at Tyburn. Educated at the English College in Rome, he was ordained priest on 10 April 1597. He came to England and, after working on the mission for some time, he was captured and sentenced to banishment from England and any of the British Dominions in 1606.

He did, however, return and was again exiled. On his third arrest for returning to England, he was sent to Newgate prison in 1611. Seven months later, he was brought to the Old Bailey for trial on the charge of high treason for being a priest and returning to England contrary to the law. On 30 May 1612, he suffered a martyr's death at Tyburn.

Thomas Hunt, whose real name was Benstead, was born in Norfolk. He entered the English College in Valladolid in 1592 and then transferred to the English College in Seville. He is the proto-martyr of these Colleges.

After ordination, he was sent to England and, being arrested, was imprisoned in Wisbech Castle. One night he escaped with five other priests and was helped and equipped by Fr Garnet, the Provincial of the Jesuits. With a fellow priest, Thomas Sprott, he travelled to Lincoln and put up at the Saracen's Head. Unfortunately, a search was being made for some persons who had committed a robbery and since the two priests were strangers in the district and unable to account for their movements, they were arrested on suspicion of being the thieves. When their luggage was searched, their Breviaries and Holy Oils were discovered. In court they were charged with being Seminary priests and traitors. Although no evidence was produced to prove this and although the two did not acknowledge that they were priests, the judge directed that they be found guilty. The two priests were hanged, drawn and quartered in Lincoln on 11 July 1600.

The Laity Collaborate

The Catholics of England needed priests for the Church to survive. As they said repeatedly, *'It's the Mass that matters'*. But priests alone could not save the Church. They were totally dependent on the laity for shelter, food, finance and particularly for the provision of a place to celebrate Mass in secret and places to hide in from the Government pursuivants. All this, many Catholic families provided at great risk to themselves. And the lay people could go to places and make contacts that was not possible for a priest, no matter how disguised he might be, or how many aliases he travelled under. This was truly a collaborative ministry in action, although that term, so frequently talked about today, was not known at that time. This was the pattern, to a greater or lesser extent and with varying success, throughout the seven counties of our Diocese.

Northamptonshire

In the reign of Elizabeth and onwards, Northamptonshire possessed some fifteen strongholds of the Faith namely, the halls of Deene, Harrowden, Rushden, Ashby St. Legers, Denton, Desborough, Drayton, Easton Neston, Little Oakley, Upper Heyford, Brampton Ash, Dingley, Kirby, and probably Teton near Ravensthorpe and Welford. In 1620, there were eleven Jesuits in addition to Secular Priests and Benedictines working in the County.

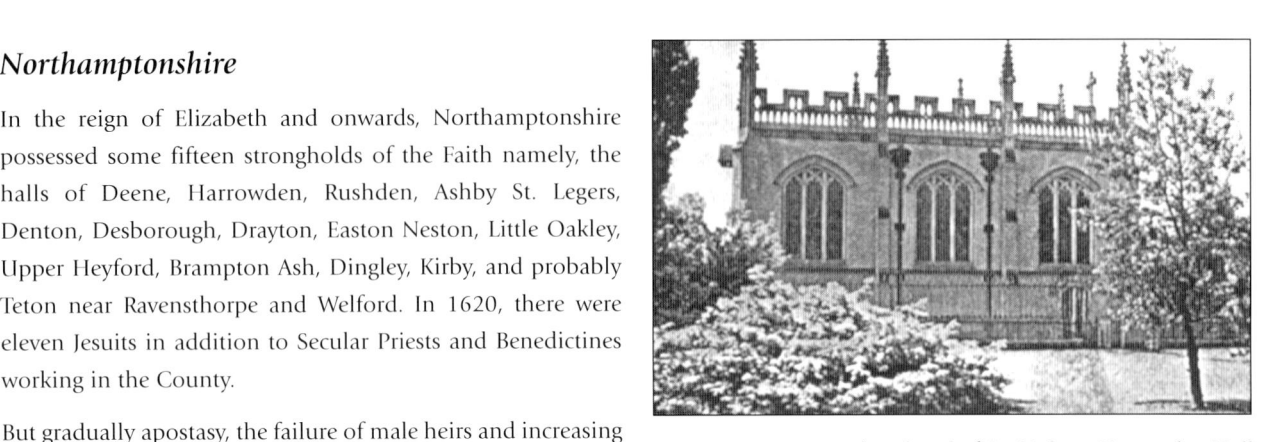

But gradually apostasy, the failure of male heirs and increasing impoverishment due to penal fines whittled all these places away

Present-day chapel of St. Hubert, Harrowden Hall

so that by 1676, when the religious census of the Archbishop of Canterbury was made, the County showed the lowest proportion of Catholics to the total population of any County within the Archbishopric. By 1750, only one priest survived on the extreme Western limit. A second had been added near the Eastern boundary by 1778, but a third did not appear until 1820.

Harrowden Hall, the property of the **Vaux** family, was one of the more famous halls of the county. Edmund Campion S.J. was there in 1580 and Lord Vaux was tried in the following year for harbouring him, Campion's alleged admissions under torture being brought in evidence against him. When John Gerard S.J. reached Harrowden in 1598, he found a priest had been living in the house for a year. Gerard made Harrowden his headquarters. The famous search of the house by a hundred men took place on 12 November 1605 and lasted nine days. Gerard was not found, although he had been in the house throughout, but two other priests, who had left earlier, ran into a cordon and were arrested.

By 1658, Lord Vaux had gone to live in Surrey and, on his death in 1661, Harrowden passed into Protestant hands until 1893, when the first Lord Vaux of the second creation bought it back.

The Poultons of Desborough provided in their house a constant Catholic centre from the death of Giles Poulton in 1558 until Ferdinand Poulton, ruined by the extravagance of his elder brother who died in 1716, was forced to part with it in 1719. The family produced no fewer than twenty-one priests.

Easton Neston (near Towcester) was acquired in about 1525 by Richard Fremor and was a Catholic house as late as 1604.

There are two places that carried the Faith forward, one from the seventeenth century to the nineteenth and the other from at least as early as 1778 to 1855.

Warkworth Manor near Banbury is just inside the Northamptonshire border. George Holman, whose father Philip had bought Warkworth earlier, became a Catholic before 1659. In 1688, George went to live at Warkworth and installed a Catholic priest there as chaplain. There was a succession of secular priest chaplains there, including Fr Alban Butler, the famous author of 'Lives of the Saints', who came there in 1751. This succession of Catholic chaplains continued into the nineteenth century.

Warkworth Manor

Overthorpe. When Francis Eyre, the owner of Warkworth, left there to live near Derby, he made provision to preserve the Catholic Faith in the neighbourhood of his old home by building a priest's house in the neighbouring village of Overthorpe. The existing church in Banbury is its direct heir, as is also the church at Aston-le-Walls.

King's Cliffe. The origin of the mission in the village of King's Cliffe, some six miles South of Stamford, is shrouded in mystery. The secular priest Anthony Barnwell was buried there in October 1778 and had died while on a visit to his brother John, also a secular priest who was therefore established by that date in what was known as the Riding Mission on account of the large area it covered. But how long he had been there, or how he came there, no one knows. No Catholic family of position owned property there, but there certainly were secular priests at King's Cliffe mission for many years. Bishop Milner confirmed at King's Cliffe in 1805 and 1812 and at Oundle in 1808 and 1817.

King's Cliffe

Northampton Town. Mass was said in the town houses of some of the Catholic families in and around Northampton. A priest was said to be living on Black Lion Hill in 1815. An advertisement in the local paper 'The Mercury' of 28 July 1821 announced that Mass will be said on Sundays in a house in Abington Street opposite the Saracen's Head. Mass was provided for the Catholic soldiers at Weedon and, in 1823, Fr Foley came to live in Northampton.

Bedfordshire

There were only three houses that provided an asylum for the Faith from 1559.

Houghton Conquest (about six miles South of Bedford). The Conquest family were recusants from at least the early seventeenth century and continued to own the house until 1741. They had resident chaplains who in the early eighteenth century were probably Benedictines.

Turvey Park was occupied by Catholic families - Mordaunt, Compton and the Earl of Peterborough - from 1504 to 1735 except for a short interlude of Protestant ownership.

Chawston Manor House. The Hunt family at Chawston was recusant from at least 1628. The resident chaplains there ceased by 1781.

Shefford. By the close of the eighteenth century the Catholic Faith was almost extinct in this County. It was carried forward into the nineteenth century by only a small group of Catholics in the little market town of Shefford.

There is a record of resident priests from about 1780 and of a congregation of five or six in 1791. A small church was built there sometime between 1791 and 1812. There were 200 Catholics in about 1830.

Buckinghamshire

There was only one house, Weston Underwood, which remained faithful to the Catholic Church from the accession of Queen Elizabeth until the end of the nineteenth century and indirectly until today, for the mission at Olney is its direct heir. Apart from this, the pattern is the usual one here of an ever diminishing number of Catholic houses throughout the sixteenth, seventeenth and eighteenth centuries and of the gradual foundation of missions from about the middle of the nineteenth.

Cambridgeshire

Cambridge University succumbed in time to the influence of the Protestant Reformers and gradually the Colleges lost their Catholic allegiance. The town and county followed a similar pattern. The area was a stronghold of Protestantism and Puritanism, especially at the time of Oliver Cromwell. This tide was resisted and the Catholic cause maintained by only two families.

The Huddleston family at Sawston Hall harboured priests at the house, especially Jesuits, including John Gerard S.J. And there was a priest's hiding place at the top of the winding stairs, which it is thought was constructed by the Jesuit lay brother, Nicholas Owen.

Linton. The Paris family were persistent recusants and their successors, the Ravencrofts and Andrews, maintained the Catholic presence there up to the end of the seventeenth century.

Huntingdonshire

There were only three families in the County that protected the Catholic Faith before Queen Elizabeth died. By the middle of the seventeenth century, there was not a single Catholic centre in the County.

Priest Hole at Sawston

Norfolk

Largely due to the work of the Jesuit John Gerard, the County contained more recusant families in the reign of Elizabeth than any of the other six counties that formed the Northampton Diocese. Many of these Catholic families persevered into the seventeenth century and some into the eighteenth. By 1800, only the Bedenfields of Oxburgh, the Jerninghams of Costessey and the Havers of Thelton remained, although they had been joined by the Howards of Buckenham Tofts, and the old home of the Tasburghs was sheltering a community of nuns.

Oxburgh Hall

Suffolk

The County shows the usual pattern of an ever diminishing number of country chaplaincies in the seventeenth century and an ever increasing number of town missions in the nineteenth. The only places that had an unbroken Catholic life from the reign of Elizabeth to the present day were Coldham and Stoke-by-Nayland.

And so we arrive back to Bishop Wareing's time, after reflecting on the long history and varying fortunes of his Catholic inheritance in this Eastern region. His 'estate' would have appeared severely diminished and, at times, to have been in danger of being entirely lost. But there were recent signs of hope. It was now the task and responsibility of Bishop Wareing and his successors to see what they could make of it for the future.

2.
The First Hundred Years
❖

A TIME TO PLANT, A TIME TO BUILD, A TIME TO REJOICE

The natives were not friendly. As a description of the reaction of Protestant England to the Restoration of the Catholic Hierarchy of England and Wales, this is a considerable understatement.

The frenzied alarm and outrage, led by the Prime Minister Lord John Russell, that was aroused by the announcement of the restoration and by Wiseman's Pastoral Letter of 7 October 1850, no doubt surprised, even startled, Archbishop Nicholas Wiseman. His life was threatened and he was urged to flee abroad.

Our Bishop, William Wareing, adjusting himself to his new role, would have been keenly aware of all this. Like thousands of others, he will have read in the Times of 19 October 1850 this fanatical and fantastical outcry.

'Is it then here in Westminster, among ourselves and by the English throne, that an Italian priest is to parcel out the spiritual dominion of this country - to employ the renegades of our National Church to restore a foreign usurpation over the consciences of men?... Such an intention must be either ludicrous or intolerable - either the delusion of some fanatical brain or treason to the constitution.'

Here were his fellow countrymen crying out about the 'Italian mission' and 'Papal aggression'. Even a cartoon in Punch hammered home the message. Wareing's homecoming was not an auspicious occasion. Bishop Wareing, however, was not cowed by this, nor would he let it pass. Instead, he promptly issued his first Pastoral Letter dated, either by chance or pointedly, 5 November 1850. Calmly, but firmly, he vindicated the Pope's action and asserted the rights to which Catholics, like all other Englishmen, were entitled.

He wrote:

"Why have the Gentiles raged and the people devised vain things? The kings of the earth have stood up and the princes have met together against the Lord and against His anointed." (Ps 2)

An anti-Papal demonstration

'Circumstances have arisen which make it necessary to lose no time in addressing to you a few plain words to vindicate the conduct of our Holy Father in the establishment of a new hierarchy for England ... We hesitate not to say that the present outbreak of indignant feeling, the violent declamation, the furious onslaught and unscrupulous misrepresentation of the public press, against the Sovereign Pontiff and ourselves, the new English Bishops, exhibit a something little short of insanity.

What then, dearly beloved, is the crime against the Crown and Majesty of England of which we have been guilty? ... The Bishop of Rome, the lawful successor of St. Peter, ... thought proper to make a certain alteration in the form of our ecclesiastical government. To deny this spiritual power, to refuse to acknowledge this spiritual supremacy of the Bishop of Rome, we need not tell you, would be to renounce our Faith and cease to be Catholics.

The laws of England are fully cognisant of this fact, and hence in tending to us the oath of allegiance, they qualify the wording of that oath so as not to compel us to deny the spiritual power and supremacy of the Holy Father. If then in the exercise of this acknowledged right, he has thought proper, for good and wise reasons, and after mature deliberation, to impart to us that more regular and canonical form of church government which exists in almost every part of the Catholic world, where is the 'assumption', where is the 'audacity', where is the 'illegality' of his conduct, so much complained of?

We are told that, by the establishment of our new hierarchy, Pope Pius IX has invaded and ignored the Queen's spiritual supremacy, and that we are equally guilty in acceding to his arrangements. Does, then, our gracious Queen expect His Holiness to believe in her spiritual supremacy? Does she even compel us to acknowledge the same? Do not our own calumniators themselves well know that during the troublesome days of the persecution, the rack and the gibbet were tried upon our forefathers in vain to compel them to acknowledge the spiritual supremacy of the sovereign? And that, should those darksome days return, we must, like them, consent to be hung, drawn and quartered rather than acknowledge that supremacy?

In making this plain and open avowal, we fear not to alarm the prejudices of the candid portion of our fellow countrymen.... We know how to render temporal obedience in things temporal to our earthly sovereign, and spiritual obedience in things spiritual to God and His Vice-Regent without letting those duties clash or interfere with each other. In making this assertion we are fully borne out by the conduct and behaviour of English Catholics for the last three-hundred years. ... A new division of the country... into certain dioceses and bishops appointed to govern their respective portions of the flock ... it is urged is virtually taking possession of the country, and disposing of the territories of Queen Victoria. It is difficult to understand how persons can be found who are serious in preferring such a charge against us. If, however, any such there be, we can solemnly assure them that no such assumption of temporal power, no claim to territorial possession or worldly property, has been contemplated in the establishment of our hierarchy. As Vicars Apostolic, formerly, we had claim but upon your voluntary donations, as Bishops in ordinary, now, we have acquired no right to a single broad acre or additional stiver, even from our flocks, much less from those who do not belong to us. ... Our fellow countrymen have been led astray by exaggerated statements and terrified by imaginary fears.

"THE THIN END OF THE WEDGE"
Daring attempt to break into a church

A cartoon in "Punch", 16 November 1850, at the time of the Papal aggression.

... Whereas we have hitherto been taunted with our foreign titles, ridiculed as mere "titulars", "creatures of the Pope" and destitute of all episcopal power and character, all these anomalies have been removed in the establishment of our hierarchy by which we have become more free, more canonically constituted, more national - and, if we may so express it, more English.

While, therefore, dearly beloved, we express our gratitude to His Holiness for the favour and distinction wherewith he has honoured us, let us fervently pray that in due time, those of our countrymen whose prejudices and jealousies have been unfairly excited, may see how they have been misled, may lay aside the groundless terrors with which they have been artfully impressed, and be generously disposed to allow us quietly to enjoy the religious liberty which they claim for themselves, and which they profess to be the birthright of every Englishman.'

The Bishop ordered that this Pastoral should be read in every church and chapel in the Diocese on the first Sunday after its reception and that after Mass the Te Deum should be said or sung in Latin or English, followed by the Prayer for the Queen.

The First Chapter of Canons

From early on in the Church's history, Bishops had had a group of clerics to help them run their dioceses. So, on 24 June 1852, Bishop Wareing appointed the Northampton Chapter of Canons. Their job was to assist the Bishop in his care for the Diocese and, on the death of the Bishop, the Chapter would succeed to his ordinary and customary jurisdiction. They would have to elect a Vicar Capitular and send up three names of a possible successor.

The first members of the Northampton Chapter were appointed by Bishop Wareing and took their stalls according to seniority in the priesthood. Frederick Charles Husenbeth was elected Provost. He was a learned man with some forty-nine books to his credit, the most important of which was the life of Bishop Milner. The Canons were John Abbot, Thomas Macquaran (Penitentiary), Seth Eccles, John Dalton, Thomas Quinliven, George Rigby, Thomas Seed, Henry Thrower, Joseph Mayland (Theologian), and John Morris.

In the first session, a letter was read from Cardinal Wiseman, summoning the Chapter to elect a procurator to attend the Provincial Synod to be held on 6 July at Oscott. Provost Husenbeth was elected. The early sessions were held in a room, formerly the upper part of the old chapel, afterwards known as the dormitory, which the Bishop gave as the Chapter Room.

The early years saw the gradual making of rules and the steady organisation of the Diocese. The Holy Father was petitioned for the Chapter Mass and Office to be said but twice a year. On 8 May 1855, it was decreed that the Chapter must meet every month and that every Chapter Mass must be said for all the Benefactors to the Chapter, living and dead. It was also decreed that, on the death of a member of the Chapter, a High Mass of Requiem should be sung at the first Chapter meeting afterwards, followed by Terce and a low Mass offered by one of the Canons for all Benefactors. At this meeting five Missionary Rectors were appointed for Cambridge, Lynn, Marlow, Norwich and Stoke-by-Nayland.

F.C. Husenbeth

In the early days, the Bishop asked the Canons to pay one shilling for breakfast and he announced that he could not engage himself to provide any other entertainment, as all could be on their way home by one o'clock.

In regard to choral dress, Propaganda in 1868 agreed that the rochet should be allowed to Canons, the cappa parva to Provosts and some further distinction to Metropolitans. Through Cardinal Wiseman the choral dress was settled and Bishop Amherst, our second

Bishop, ordered the Canons to provide, as soon as possible, the dress appointed by the Holy See, even to the smallest detail of form and material. An interesting detail, the origin of which is unknown, is the custom of Northampton Canons wearing a ring at Chapter functions.

And so the Canons began their work with the Bishop of organising and building up the Diocese.

The Early Years

Schools

Over the first hundred years, many schools were built in the Diocese and many of them were started by Religious Orders. The convent and school of Notre Dame in Northampton was one of the first of these and its history may serve as an example of the development and subsequent fortunes of other such schools. In 1845, a small community of nuns of the Congregation of the Infant Jesus from Nivelles in Brabant came to Northampton and were installed in number 55 Sheep Street. Their work included Day and Sunday Schools, evening instructions for women and girls, a workroom for poor girls and the nucleus of the Boarding Schools of later years.

In 1846, the Convent was separated from its Mother House and, in 1848, it moved to a building that was later part of the sacristy of the Cathedral. This building was by no means ideal, but it at least had more air and space than the little house in Sheep Street. In 1851, there was the opportunity of acquiring three houses in Abington Street, then a pleasant residential district with large gardens and fields nearby.

Notre Dame School, Northampton

But sometime later, a terrible malignant typhus broke out among the Sisters. The Boarders returned to their homes and the Sisters dispersed. Three of the Sisters died within a week and a fourth after lingering for a few weeks. The other Sisters, who had been less seriously ill, gradually recovered. When all fear of infection had passed, the Sisters returned and friends helped them with the heavy debts that had been incurred.

Since they were isolated from their Mother House, the Superioress and her Counsellors felt that their house needed to be placed on a solid footing. It was suggested that they should join with the Sisters of Notre Dame of Namur. Bishop Wareing and the Bishop of Namur approved this plan and, on 8 October 1852, the union was completed.

As time went on, the three houses in Abington Street were not considered large enough for the increasing number of children and so, in 1870-71, work was begun to erect a new building on the site of these houses.

The Education Act of 1870 made it necessary to build an elementary school for the number of children now compelled to attend school. As a result the Sisters, in 1872-73, built St. Mary's School on part of the garden opening on to The Mounts. At first this building accommodated boys, girls and infants. In 1880, the boys were moved to a new building in

Clare Street. In 1890, the property adjoining the convent was acquired and a fine new building was erected to provide accommodation for both day and boarding schools, until further extensions were required in 1922. In 1938, the extensive new wing, known as Our Lady's building, was begun. This comprised modern Kindergarten and Preparatory classrooms and cloakrooms, with a lofty, spacious Assembly Hall for dramatic performances. It is estimated that at the peak period nearly a thousand children attended the school. A Science Block and Domestic Science room were added in 1950.

Already, in 1945, the school had been accepted as a Direct-Grant Grammar School, but to meet the requirements of the Board of Education and provide the specialised rooms essential to a Grammar School, the boarding school was closed. In 1952, the School numbered two hundred in the Kindergarten and Preparatory School and four hundred and fifty in the Upper School.

Since then, the situation, both in education and in the Religious Orders, has changed. There were fewer Sisters available to staff the school and the Comprehensive School System had come in. In the mid-Seventies, Notre Dame School was closed. The Sisters left Northampton and the school and convent building were demolished. The pupils joined with a Catholic Secondary Modern School to form the new comprehensive St. Thomas Becket Catholic Upper School. The Abington Street site is now occupied by Marks and Spencer and similar high-street shops. This history of the Notre Dame School in Northampton is, in many ways, a paradigm of the course of Catholic education in general over the past one hundred and fifty years - small, difficult beginnings often pioneered by Religious Orders; then more lay involvement and in recent times the progressive withdrawal of Religious from many schools; constant efforts to meet the mounting requirements of the State Education Authorities; and always the urgent and unrelenting need to raise the large sums of money required.

All ten Bishops of Northampton, over the past one hundred and fifty years, have made the provision of Catholic schools a prime concern and they have evoked a generous, and at times sacrificial, response from the laity.

Social Care

Bishop Amherst was aware that, as well as Catholic education, another pressing concern was the provision of care for orphan children and for poor, aged and infirm people.

Already, in 1868, Canon Collis in Shefford had opened a Diocesan Orphanage dedicated to St. Francis in a house adjoining the priest's house. In time, this would develop and, much later, be transformed into the St. Francis Children's Society. But for the moment, Bishop Amherst saw that something more was needed.

In 1875, he turned for help to the Poor Sisters of Nazareth. This community had been founded in Hammersmith in 1851 under the guidance and with the support of Cardinal Wiseman and received the first approval of the Holy See in 1899.

The Bishop warned the Foundress, Mother Basil, and her companion, when they met him to discuss the matter, that the foundation in Northampton would be difficult, because the people were poor and prejudiced. Mother Basil was not put off by this and, trusting in Divine Providence, set out to look for a suitable house.

At first the Sisters rented an unfurnished house in St. George's Terrace with Mother Agnes Burke as Superior. Very soon the house was filled with orphan children and a larger place was needed. So the Sisters searched for a plot of land on which to build a house suited to their work. When no available site could be found, the Bishop sold them a plot next to the

Cathedral. The Sisters were grateful for this, but it meant that they had to trim their plans as the area was restricted. They built their house there in 1878.

At first, the Sisters laboured under severe hardships as their means were very meagre. Sometimes the Sisters (two) out on quest all day would return in the evening with very little food or money. Later on, however, when the work of the Sisters became better known, people were very supportive.

The Sisters have persevered and still have a house in Northampton. They moved from the house near the Cathedral to a new site further out in 1960 and now continue to care for the aged and infirm there.

Opening of the new Nazareth House

Catholic Life

The Cathedral, the Bishop, Canons, particular projects of Religious Orders, such as a school or an orphanage are, of course, all important. But they are only part of the picture of the Diocese in those early years. Fortunately, we can get at least a glimpse of Diocesan life and concerns then from the pages of the first issue of the 'Northampton Catholic Magazine' 1869 vol. 1. No. 1.

This magazine, which was discovered by chance in a presbytery in 1952, was published with the stated aim of 'supplying a means of communication between the various Missions of the Diocese'.

We get an indication of the general outlook and concerns of Catholics then from the magazine's contents. The sixteen pages of a monthly issue are almost entirely devoted to religious articles. They are mostly of a controversial nature, to demonstrate the errors of the Protestant Church. For instance, 'The Fruits of the Catholic and Protestant Doctrine'; 'Mistakes about Infallibility'; 'Married or Unmarried' refers to the Clergy; 'The Meaning of Benediction' (in those days not so frequent as it was later); the beginning of 'Quarant' Ore' in the Diocese as a new devotion.

Quite a number of articles deal with the very prevalent vice of drunkenness. As its circulation widened, non-Catholics wrote controversial letters. Intolerance was rife, as is clear in that whenever new Missions were started they provoked local demonstrations of opposition.

In a subscription list for the Jubilee of Pope Pius IX, thirty Missions are recorded. The highest subscription, of £15 - 16 - 9, was from Salt Hill (which now means Slough). Another strange name is Landguard Fort, which is probably Felixstowe. In those days it was served from Harwich.

The Cathedral of Bishop Amherst had then only been completed four years, and Peterborough, Weedon and Aston-le-Walls were the only Missions in the county of Northampton with resident priests.

Wellingborough Mission was in the earliest days of its infancy. A start had been made, in August 1868, in a 'small hired room for the benefit of the few Catholics resident in the town and the neighbouring villages'. In 1869, 'a larger and more commodious place' (which we now know to have been two rooms in 12 Church Street) had been fitted up as a chapel dedicated to Our Lady of the Sacred Heart for the faithful 'expected from the large and increasing ironstone works'. The beginnings had been made by Canon Scott from the Cathedral, but later it was in the charge of Fr Bernard Murray. The Cathedral Choir, owing to 'the great railway convenience', was giving occasional help and the opening of the Chapel was attended by violent attacks in the local press, 'with the unerring instinct of heresy ... upon Her between whom and itself God had placed enmity from the beginning'.

Bedford and Wolverton Missions are also mentioned as being in similar straits. Fr G.F. Stokes at Wolverton had a completed church, but was suffering actual physical persecution by mobs enraged by the notorious renegade Murphy, whose diatribes caused disturbances in many places in the Diocese and even in Newport Pagnell, Olney and Market Harborough, 'in some of which places there is not a single Catholic'.

Weston Underwood, Wisbech, Coldham Cottage and Norwich receive notices in 'Parish News' as flourishing Missions. Fr Copeland at 'Thorney Bar' or High Fen, like Fr Warmoll at Bedford, had just completed a small permanent church. Cambridge, 'this most important Mission' had not only new schools 'to replace the small and inconvenient ones soon found insufficient', but also was looking forward to the erection of a 'church worthy of the faith of St. Andrew and the noble memories of the ancient and formerly Catholic seat of learning'.

St. Francis Home, Shefford, began in this year and received considerable notice in the magazine. The central part of the Home was reconstructed to take fifty boys and Canon Collis, in November 1869, appealed for a further £600 for furnishings.

The picture we get is of a Catholic community that is growing and building, but also that is coming out more into the light of national life and with a certain self-confidence. It all sounds very hopeful.

St Francis' Home, Shefford

Planting and Building - Missions; Stations; Chapels. (1880-1907)

Rt. Rev Arthur Riddell was Bishop of Northampton from 1880 to 1907 and this period was also remarkable for the number of Missions and Mass Stations that were opened and Chapels that were built.

We do not, at this date, speak of Parishes, because until 1908 England was still regarded as a missionary country under the direction of Propaganda in Rome. It was only in 1918 that Canonical Parishes were created and the post of Missionary Rectors ceased.

A Mission is an area where the local Catholics have provision for Mass and the Sacraments and generally a resident priest and where there may or may not be a chapel.

A Mass Station would not have a resident priest and the Mass would generally be celebrated at somebody's residence, or a public oratory in a large house.

The chapels that were built might be a temporary structure. Bishop Riddell speaks of aiming for chapels *'of moderate size, but of good design in new centres'*.

Bishop Riddell

An early church

Opening of Missions

Date	Place	First Resident Priest
18. 10. 1880	Sudbury	Valerius D'Apreda
15. 12. 1880	Daventry	Thomas Fitzgerald
30. 4. 1881	Woodbridge *(subsequently given up and served from Ipswich)*	George Wilmot Mayne
1. 5. 1881	Lowestoft	G. Brennan
21. 7. 1881	Wellingborough	B. Murray
29. 9. 1881	Lynford	M. Dwane
20. 1. 1884	Luton	Joseph O'Connor
4. 11. 1885	Slough	Joseph Clemente
8. 9. 1888	Brampton *(given up Nov. 1890 on closing of the school)*	Francis Laborde
7. 12. 1888	Aylesbury	James Collins
3. 7. 1889	Gorleston	Edward Scott
3. 11. 1889	High Wycombe	Herbert Beale
July 1890	Ely	J. Freeland
20. 9. 1891	Kettering	Henry Stanley
2. 7. 1892	Buckingham	Fr Thaddeus O.F.M.
31. 10. 1895	Leighton Buzzard	Charles Reilly
Aug 1899	Felixstowe	William Cooper
1899	Southwold	Henry St. Leger Mason
1899	St. George Norwich	Henry Long
1899	Olney *(to succeed Weston Underwood)*	Carton de Wiart
31. 8. 1902	Rushden	James Shore
Sept 1902	Cromer	T. Walmsley Carter
Nov 1903	Hunstanton	Ernest Garnett
June 1905	Fakenham	H. Gray
2. 6. 1906	Woodbridge	Charles Reilly

Stations Opened

Date	Station	Served From	Place
1881	Bradwell	Lowestoft	At Mr Smith's
30 June 1882	Catton	St. John Norwich	Public Oratory at residence of Sperling Esq.
1882	Pin Mill	St. Pancras Ipswich	
9 Sept 1883	Brooke House	St. John Norwich	public oratory.
1885	Aylesbury	Wolverton	at house of Mr Roche
1885	Quidenham Hall	St. John Norwich	pub. or. at residence Viscount Bury.
1885	Ditton Park	Slough	pub. or. at residence of Duchess of Buccleuch.
1885	Sennow (*instead of Brooke*)		pub.or. at residence of Mrs Exsham.
23 Sept 1886	Hothorpe	Husbands Bosworth	pub. or. at residence of R. De Trafford.
17 Oct 1886	Gissing Hall	Holy Apostles Norwich	pub. or. at residence of S. Harwood.
1889	Rayners. High Wycombe	High Wycombe	pub. or. at residence of Sir Philip Rose.
1889	Gillingham Hall	Beccles	pub. or. at residence of John Kenyon.
1890	The Hyde, Luton	Luton	pub. or. at residence of Viscount Bury.
1891	Cattawade	East Bergholt	pub. or.
1892	Leighton Buzzard	Wolverton	pub. or.
1895	Dunstable	Luton	pub. or.
1900	St. Ives	Cambridge	pub. or.
1905	Biggleswade	Shefford	pub. or.

Chapels Opened

8 Aug	1898	Gillingham
6 Aug	1899	Felixstowe
10 June	1900	St. Ives (*wooden chapel*)
18 Nov	1900	Olney
4 June	1901	Huntingdon
9 Sept	1901	Beccles (*nave and aisles*)
5 June	1902	Lowestoft (*church*)
9 June	1902	St. Ives (*church from Cambridge*)
18 Dec	1902	Nayland (*church*)
21 Oct	1903	Ely (*church*)
21 July	1904	Hunstanton (*church*)
5 Mar	1905	Rushden (*chapel*)
19 Mar	1905	Peterley (*chapel, brick and wood*)
24 Nov	1905	Harrowden

Around The Diocese

In 1895

In Bedfordshire, Bishop Riddell confirmed at Shefford, Leighton Buzzard and Luton. In Leighton Buzzard there was a Catholic community of about forty-five, of whom twenty-one attended Mass, provided by the priest at Wolverton. A gift of £25 a year from a parishioner, a Mrs White, enabled the Bishop to send Fr Charles Reilly to the town on 31 October with instructions, 'to foster the congregation and to build a church and presbytery'.

On 20 October, Mass was said for the first time since the Reformation at Dunstable, but in the absence of any benefactor the small community had to wait until 1927 for regular church sevices. Meanwhile they walked to Luton for Mass.

In Northamptonshire, at Hothorpe, just North of Kettering, the little church built by Charles Edmund Trafford, with a congregation of fifteen, was visited by the Bishop who was called upon to bless the new bell.

In Cambridgeshire, Bishop Riddell also blessed the nine bells in the new church in Cambridge. These were cast by Messrs Taylor of Loughborough who cast the great bell at St. Paul's, London. The tenor bell in the new church was reputed to be the largest in Cambridgeshire. The clock chimed the quarters on the bells, to the tune of the 'Alleluia', day and night on Holy Saturday - much to the disturbance of the neighbourhood - until they became accustomed to the sound. The Angelus (eighteen strokes on the same note) was rung three times a day. The bells were an appropriate way of celebrating Rome's decision to allow Catholic students to attend English universities from this year.

In Norfolk, Bishop Riddell confirmed at Norwich, Yarmouth and Wroxham Hall. Of the Catholic population in the county of three thousand, two and a half thousand resided in Norwich and Yarmouth. The remaining five hundred were scattered across the countryside. Wroxham had a Catholic population of nine, Lynford of thirty-seven. There was no Catholic Mission on the coast from King's Lynn to Yarmouth, a distance of eighty miles. Bishop Riddell bought a piece of land in the developing seaside resort of Cromer to provide services for summer visitors and a small church was formally opened by Canon Duckett on 25 August. A curate from Norwich travelled to Cromer to say Mass throughout the summer. At Norwich the Bishop inspected the first part of the new church of St. John's and approved plans to convert the church in Willow Lane into new schools for the five hundred and fifty children in the town.

In Northampton, on 15 December, Bishop Riddell celebrated the twenty-fifth anniversary of the proclamation recognising St. Joseph as the Patron Saint of the Catholic Church by singing High Mass - with pomp and ceremony - at the Cathedral.

At Peterborough, after many years of effort, the foundation stone was laid by Bishop Riddell for a new and larger church. He preached a sermon on St. Peter and his glory in pre-Reformation times, especially in Peterborough. The congregation was urged to remain faithful to the spirit of Catholics in the past and the service ended with the singing of 'Faith of our Fathers'. The old church had already been sold and for the rest of the year the school was used as a temporary church. The infant school was turned into the Sanctuary.

At Ditton Park, Slough, the Dowager Duchess of Buccleuch died on 28 March. A convert, she was regarded as the founder of the Kettering mission (a town she described as 'being full of dissenters of every description and very little Catholic') and an important benefactor of Fr Clemente of Slough. She provided for two schools in the town and her aid was sorely missed. After her death, Fr Clemente was forced to advertise in London papers for pupils in Italian and French in order to supplement his meagre income.

Church of Our Lady and the English Martyrs, Cambridge

Mrs Lyne Stephens, benefactress.

In Suffolk, at Sudbury, a mission comprising two towns and eight villages, the small congregation mourned the death of its priest, Fr William Tippard, who died of consumption on 24 January at Southampton. During his three years at Sudbury he had increased the number of practising Catholics from thirty-five to over one hundred and built a new church. As the Sunday offerings seldom exceeded five shillings, most of the money was raised by Fr Tippard from national and local appeals. His exertions wore him out and his death at the age of thirty-two was a sore loss to the Diocese.

In 1896

At the beginning of 1896, Bishop Riddell set out on his 'ad limina' visit to Rome, a journey of seventeen days by steam train. In Rome he visited the Shrines of St. Peter and St. Paul and presented to Pope Leo XIII an account of the Diocese. In the four years since his last visit there had been five hundred and seventy conversions in the seven counties, bringing the total number of church members to 10,469, less than the number of Catholics in Corby today.

The Pope granted his Apostolic Blessing to the people of the Diocese and in return, in his Pastoral Letter, the Bishop asked them to pray for the Pope, facing problems created by nationalistic forces, especially in Italy. Europe seemed to be fragmenting into warring nations intent on founding 'Empires'. Britain had sent Kitchener to Sudan, with Fr Wallace from Ipswich serving as a military chaplain. Back home, Bishop Riddell began a series of visitations.

In Buckinghamshire, he visited the two new missions of Aylesbury and High Wycombe to inspect their progress. In 1888, there were 30 Catholics in Aylesbury and little money for the mission, but by 1896 Fr James Collins had managed to erect an iron chapel with money lent by the Bishop, and the congregation had increased to 124. In nearby High Wycombe a mission had also been founded. It was fortunate in finding a benefactor in Sir Philip Rose from Penn, four miles away. By 1896, a congregation of 114 was established and an aisle and chapel of a stone church had been built. In September, the congregation was kept busy learning plainchant from Fr Drake from Slough so that sung Masses could take place. The Bishop commended the congregations for their progress and set mission boundaries. Aylesbury was to be responsible for Princes Risborough, Little Hampden, Great Missenden and the Cheyneys; High Wycombe for Hampden, Little Missenden, Chalfont St. Peters, Beaconsfield and Booker.

In Suffolk, Bishop Riddell confirmed in Ipswich, the Benedictine missions at Bungay and Beccles on the river Waveney and the Jesuit foundation at Bury St. Edmunds. He also visited the domestic chapel at Yaxley Hall near Eye, which was served from Lowestoft. In September, the first Mass was said in Haverhill in the Bell Hotel by Fr Donovan from Kirtling Towers, but no regular services were to take place for many years.

In Norfolk, Fr Michael Vernon died at Wroxham Hall in June, aged 68. He had performed most of his priestly ministry as the private chaplain of the Squire of Wroxham on his estate in the Broads. A new church, St. George's Fishergate, in Norwich was blessed by the Bishop in September; an old charity school was refurbished to serve as a church with money provided by the late Earl of Orford and the Duke of Norfolk. The Bishop also opened the new public elementary school in the city, made necessary by the condemnation of the two existing schools by the Education Department. The old chapel in Willow Lane, built in 1829 in a Classical style, was converted into a school for 555 pupils. Among other changes, the chapel was converted into the central hall, the gallery was moved and an upper floor built. The altar was taken to the new church at Cromer on the coast.

Willow Lane Chapel, Norwich.

Bishop Riddel then travelled to King's Lynn where the small Gothic church, designed by A.W.Pugin in 1845, had to be pulled down as its foundations had given way. The walls had cracked from top to bottom, the roof had opened in two places and one of the windows was out of perpendicular. The poor Catholics at the mission, numbering less than 100, had no money for the rebuilding and so the money had to be raised by subscription and public appeals through the press. Fifty guineas were given by the Prince of Wales as the church served his Catholic guests at Sandringham on Sundays and Holy Days. It took ten years to raise half the £1,200 needed and the foundation stone was able to be laid. It was planned to erect a shrine to Our Lady of Walsingham in the new church, as Walsingham was part of this extensive mission.

In Peterborough, the high point of the year was the opening of the church of All Souls, on 15 October, although the church was hardly finished. The interior was still bare, with a temporary altar and no colour except the makeshift altar hangings and a red Sanctuary carpet. It looked and felt cold and the bare boards made a resounding noise. The truncated aisle was closed by a brick wall with a door placed in it and a small wooden lean-to to serve as a porch. A further £1,500 was needed to finish the church and a series of children's plays and musical entertainments was organised by the new curate, Fr Cary-Elwes (an accomplished cellist), to raise the money.

All Souls' Church, Peterborough

Meanwhile, all the Diocesan clergy and a large congregation gathered for a busy day of ceremonies. In the morning, the walls of the church were blessed and there was a grand, Pontifical High Mass sung by the Bishop. At two o'clock there was a public luncheon in the Grand Assembly Rooms for over 100 people with 'excellent speaking'. In the evening, came Pontifical Benediction preceded by the blessing of the statue of St. Peter.

In Cambridge, provision had to be made for the spiritual welfare of Catholic students entering the University for the first time since the Protestant Reformation. The secular students were provided with a chaplain, Fr Edmund Nolan, appointed by the newly founded Universities Catholic Education Board and a lecturer, the Rev E.C. Butler, was invited to give lectures on Catholic philosophy, history and religious knowledge. For ordained students, two houses of study were founded, St. Benet's for the English Benedictines and St. Edmund's for the Secular Clergy, provided by the Duke of Norfolk. These two buildings were blessed by the Bishop in November.

In 1897

The major event in 1897 was Queen Victoria's Diamond Jubilee in June. This developed into a National Day of Thanksgiving for the advances made in the last sixty years. Cardinal Vaughan, the Archbishop of Westminster, proposed as specific reasons for thankfulness the Queen's example of personal virtue, integrity and service, the improvement in comfort, health and general culture due to advances in science and education and the increasing community spirit uniting rich and poor through Christian charity. (The Diamond Jubilee Fund raised three quarters of a million pounds for hospitals.)

The Very Rev Mgr Canon Edmund Nolan (1857-1931), Chaplain at Cambridge 1896-1902

The Cardinal gave especial thanks that under the aegis of civil and religious liberty there had been a decline in the 'unreasoning prejudice' against the Catholic Church and that Catholics were now trusted like other subjects of the Crown. This acceptance was illustrated by the part played by Catholics in the June celebrations. On Sunday 20th, a Te Deum was sung, or said in all Catholic Churches for the blessings of the Queen's reign. Bishop Riddell witnessed the Jubilee procession from Buckingham Palace to St. Paul's Cathedral on the 22nd, and on the next day, which was set aside for children's celebrations, Cardinal Vaughan presented an Address to the Queen on behalf of all Catholic schools.

Away from the euphoria of public celebrations, unobtrusive events in this year were fashioning Diocesan activity for the next fifty years. On a sunny 19 August, a pilgrimage to

First revived Shrine of Our Lady of Walsingham, King's Lynn, 1897

Our Lady of Walsingham took place at King's Lynn, the nearest Catholic Church to the Shrine destroyed at the Protestant Reformation. It was organised by the Parish Priest, Fr George Wrigglesworth, and Fr Philip Fletcher of the Guild of Our Lady of Ransom. The pilgrims processed to the King's Lynn railway station to collect the new statue of Our Lady, chosen and blessed by Pope Leo XIII to replace the one destroyed three hundred years earlier. The new statue was based on a picture in the Church of St. Maria in Cosmedin in Rome and carved in wood at Oberammergau. The pilgrims, reciting the Rosary, carried the statue to the new Catholic Church in London Road, King's Lynn, pausing at the remains of the mediaeval Chapel of Our Lady of the Red Mount on the way. The statue was enthroned in the new Lady Chapel, which had been specifically designed as a replica of the former Walsingham Shrine. The next day, the pilgrims walked to Walsingham and held a short service outside the former Slipper Chapel. The Shrine at King's Lynn became the scene of annual pilgrimages to Our Lady until 1934, when the Shrine was at last restored to Walsingham.

In Suffolk, the 35 Catholics in the small fishing port of Southwold were grateful at last to have a chapel of their own. Mr James Crimmon, at his own expense, furnished a room in the grounds of the Manor House, which was blessed on 7 June and dedicated to St. Peter. With his brother he pledged £25 a year towards the upkeep of a priest and when Fr Henry St. Leger Mason was ordained at Lisbon in March, he was sent by Bishop Riddell to serve the new mission. He was to remain there until his death in 1940 and with a sympathetic, though small, congregation he managed to build a church and presbytery and take an active part in the town's affairs. He became a member of the Council and the local Literary Society and established a lending library for the town. In the nineteen-twenties, with Canon Davidson at Aldeburgh, he initiated the Guild of St. Felix and the Dunwich pilgrimage in honour of St. Felix which became part of the Diocesan Calendar. Dunwich, four miles South West of Southwold, had been the Episcopal See of St. Felix, later an important mediaeval port, but it had been engulfed by the sea and the remains are now submerged three miles out at sea.

The 34 Catholics in the Bedfordshire town of Leighton Buzzard were also provided, at last,

Dunwich Pilgrimage

with their own place of worship. Fr Charles Reilly, who had been resident in the town since 1895, had steadily managed to raise £250 to buy a plot of land in Beaudesert Road and purchased an iron hut, which was opened as a temporary church on 16 December. The permanent church was finally opened in 1953.

The more numerous Catholic community in Slough were enriched by the arrival of the Bernardine Nuns from Lille Esquernes, Belgium, who took up residence in the town on 7 July. They opened a boarding school for girls on 6 October, specialising in English and French and also opened a small day school for the parish. They took on the task of organising parish activities, guilds, including the Guild of Our Lady and catechism classes. Fr Drake was sent from Shefford to act as their chaplain and to aid Fr Clemente in his parish work.

After years of patient waiting and hopeful fund-raising, Bishop Riddell was at last able to sanction an extension of the Diocesan Orphanage for Boys at Shefford, which had been begun in 1869 in some ramshackle premises and had been improved piecemeal ever since. The new improvements, which cost £1,349 with an additional £150 for cooking apparatus, consisted of a large kitchen, a scullery and drying room, a pantry and store rooms, a matron's room and a boiler room and some baths. Upstairs there was a new and well ventilated dormitory with a master's room and a walk-in wardrobe. Fundraising was recommenced throughout the Diocese to provide for the further improvements required to bring the Home up to a reasonable standard.

In 1898

Scientific discoveries and technological advances this year were to change fundamentally the way that the natural world was understood and lead directly to the technological age of the twentieth century. This age needed a literate and numerate workforce and there was a continuing struggle over education between the Churches and the Government. The Christian Churches were united in their belief that they should have some say in the education of children to ensure that education would take place within a moral framework. In a joint Pastoral Letter, the Bishops of England urged support for the Catholic Schools Committee. They asked every family to give at least a penny on the Feast of the Sacred Heart to support the organisation. Since 1843, it had attempted to maintain training colleges, provide religious inspection of schools, assist poor schools with buildings and grants and to liaise with Government on educational matters. By 1896, there were 295,084 children on the register of Catholic schools.

The Diocesan Synod was held in July and was attended by fifty-two priests. In his speech, Bishop Riddell thanked them for their untiring labours and self-sacrifice in helping him in his pastoral work. He mentioned especially their duties in visiting parishioners and providing for the education of children. In a parish with no school, they were asked to provide catechism classes on Thursdays and to impress on parents their responsibility as the first instructors of their children. In reaction to the increased use of bicycles, the clerical coat was allowed to be 'slightly shortened'. The clergy were advised to 'observe due moderation as of speed' to lessen the chance of accidents, remembering how short of priests the Diocese was.

The second Diocesan pilgrimage to King's Lynn occurred in June, attended by about two hundred pilgrims. In the sermon, Fr Freeland called attention to the fact that in the Gospels Mary was to be found alongside her Son throughout his life and ministry from Nazareth to Calvary, his Resurrection and Ascension into heaven. This was accepted by the Church for fifteen hundred years and the knowledge was lost in the sixteenth century. It was the work of his hearers and himself to introduce England again to the Blessed Virgin Mary and he asked as many as possible to say a prayer at the little shrine.

In the small, poor mission of Leighton Buzzard, which also served Dunstable eight miles away, Fr Reilly at last succeeded in having a presbytery built next to the iron chapel. For four hundred pounds it was a small house of six rooms with a garden and fruit trees.

The trend of relocating centres of Catholic worship in the developing towns from country houses was illustrated within the Diocese this year, though some private oratories were to provide a focus for worship in rural districts into the next century. In December, the Throckmorton estate at Weston Underwood, which had provided a place for worship throughout the Penal times, was sold, including the chapel, presbytery and school. The Catholic population of one hundred and six were now spiritually homeless and in 1899 would have to begin again at Olney, one and a quarter miles away.

The death of Mrs Arkwright at Knuston Hall near Irthlingborough, in November, led to the closure of the oratory there and the church furniture was handed over to Canon Murray for the use of the new mission in Rushden. She had been a benefactor of the Wellingborough mission in its infancy, paying for a priest to come from Northampton and a room to be hired for Mass.

The estate at Lynford Hall in Norfolk was sold in December, but the little church built by Mrs Lyne Stephens did not pass out of Diocesan hands and a resident priest had been provided for by her. So this remote corner of Norfolk was not deprived of the Sacraments.

Families still aided the founding of new missions in rural areas. In October, Harrowden Hall in Northants was bought by Lord Vaux and he intended to provide an oratory when he took up residence.

At Gillingham Hall in Norfolk, a new church was opened in August in the churchyard adjoining the road to Loddon and Norwich. It was paid for by Mr J.G. Kenyon of Gillingham Hall and the church was to be served by the Benedictines from Bungay who had also founded a mission in Beccles.

In September, an untiring and intrepid priest, Fr Job Wallace of Ipswich, died. A convert from Anglicanism, he was a great benefactor to the congregation of Ipswich. He provided St. Pancras church with a High Altar, Stations of the Cross and stained glass windows and gave the money for the school buildings. For the tiny congregation at Woodbridge, he purchased a piece of land in Crown Place on which a church was built at his expense. A man of great learning, while in Ipswich he gave lessons in Latin and Greek at the Convent School. From Ipswich, he went out as military chaplain in the Ashanti wars (1873), nursing in the fever hospitals on the coast. He later went to Madras on the missions for two years and then to Burma as military chaplain. Then he went to Omaha, Nabraska, with the first 'settlers'. His life was marked by a spirit of absolute unworldliness and self-sacrifice, especially for the sick and poor.

Church of Our Lady of Consolation and St. Stephen, Lynford

In 1899

Events in the Diocese highlighted some of its poor and most isolated missions. In June, Fr William Cooper was sent to his life's work as the first post-Reformation Catholic priest in Felixstowe with 'two bags and the Bishop's blessing'. There were then six Catholics known in the town and ten residing at Landguard Fort (which guarded the entrance to Harwich), but the town was developing as a summer watering place and Fr Cooper was to provide regular services for the visitors.

Treated at the beginning with vague suspicion, he could find nowhere to stay and so he cycled daily from Ipswich to say Mass over an ice cream shop in the Orwell Road. Eventually he managed to find a house in Gainsborough Road, whose main feature was a ladder in place of a staircase to go upstairs by. A plot of land was acquired by August and a small church with seats for 80 was opened. This was always inadequate for the summer months and visitors were to be seen kneeling outside during Mass. Slowly the early hostility gave way to friendliness and the congregation increased.

In July, Fr Francis Warmoll died, aged 49, at Stowmarket, twelve miles from Ipswich. He was buried there quietly after serving the town for twenty years. In that time the congregation had increased in number from 6 to 55, scattered over a large area. The small iron church (24 x 12 feet), which had doubled as a day school, had been replaced by a school-chapel at a cost of £1,600. The school room was downstairs and the chapel above it. The money was raised by a series of charity appeals in national newspapers and with the help of distant friends. Fr Warmoll supported himself by undertaking private tutoring. After his death, the school had to be closed due to lack of funds. The new priest, Fr O'Hagen, planned to open it as soon as possible.

In October, on the coast at Southwold, the 46 Catholics at last had a resident priest and regular church services. Since 1897, Fr Henry St. Leger Mason had travelled from Lowestoft. Now at last he was able to rent a house for £19 a year. He was to remain at Southwold for forty years and see a church and presbytery built.

Changes took place in Buckinghamshire this year when the congregation of 106 at Weston Underwood found itself homeless after the sale of the estate. The chapel, presbytery and school were given up in March. The last Mass was said on 25 March by Fr Carton de Wiart. The altar was then pulled down and the congregation was invited to remove their belongings. The next day, Fr de Wiart said Mass in Olney, one and a quarter miles away above Mr Glasspole's chemist shop in the High Street. A week later, he took up lodgings in the same premises which were cramped and made noisy by, among other things, electric bells from the shop and screams from the dentist's room. A hall was speedily found which could be used for Sunday Mass. It had been recently used as a laundry and a dancing room. Mass was celebrated here at a temporary altar after a week of cleaning, painting and decorating by Fr de Wiart and his helpers. About 50 people attended both the morning and evening services. Land was now needed to build a permanent church and presbytery and to this end Fr de Wiart drew on his private income and undertook a series of begging tours in Belgium.

The congregation at Beecles was also planning a new church. The foundation stone was laid by Dr Duckett on 26 April. He asked for prayers that God would enable them to finish the work. So far, £7,000 had been raised from unknown benefactors, but more was still needed. The church was to be named after St. Benedict, whose followers had done so much to rekindle the faith along the Norfolk-Suffolk border from the centre at Bungay.

Into the Twentieth Century

The last two decades of the nineteenth century for the Diocese, under the guidance of Bishop Riddell, had indeed been a time of planting new Missions and building new Chapels and Churches. The number is remarkable. In addition, the Catholic population and the number of priests had increased. The Diocese could now feel that it was restored and established.

We should hardly expect such expansion and building to continue at that pace. Nor did it. The picture of the Diocese in the first thirty years of the twentieth century was markedly different. Bishop Keating (1908-21) differed in many ways from his predecessor and had

Bishop Keating

different priorities. For instance, although he consecrated several churches that Bishop Riddell had inaugurated, he established far fewer than had Bishop Riddell.

Life in the Diocese was now more settled even, it might be said, more ordinary. We get some idea of what this was like in the years leading up to the First World War from the pages of the Diocesan Magazine - 'The St. Francis Magazine' *(published from Shefford in aid of the Boys' Home)*. It gives a sense of the measured and orderly progress of parish life, uninterrupted except by the occasional transfer of a priest. Although life for Catholics seems to have been hard and poor, there is also evidence of a robust and sure religion. One recent commentator on this period writes, *'Untouched by thought of "change", strongly imbued with their own Penal history, unused to travel, convinced of the permanence of the social strata then prevailing, seemingly straightforward and uncynical, the Catholics of Northampton Diocese pursued a dogged, but unruffled course. Mention is seldom made of new Missions being opened. The overall impression is that of retrenchment, defence of the True Faith, with the little flock in each town close-knit and independent in its amusements as in its devotions'.*

Although the Catholic population had increased, Catholics were still a minority and keenly aware of their Protestant neighbours and with an interest in apologetics and making converts. In January 1914, Bishop Keating said that, with a Catholic population of 14,899, Northampton remained the smallest Diocese numerically with the exception of Menevia. Clifton with Bristol, Plymouth with its 'three towns' and Nottingham with its manufacturing centres were keeping well ahead. *'We have little to hope for'*, said the Bishop, *'from immigration, while migration and emigration are a constant drain. Growth will never be ours by "luck", only by sheer perseverance.'* There was one priest for every 180 Catholics, but those Catholics were widely scattered. The Diocese, however, was strong in conversions: thirty-four per cent of Baptisms were receptions into the Church.

It seems that the pageantry of Catholic ritual was of tremendous importance to the Catholics at that time and Confirmations, for example, were reported on in every rubrical detail. There are frequent accounts of the installation of organs in churches and of the ambitious repertoire of sung Masses and enthusiastic choirs. It is interesting that money-raising was often done by means of concerts in which Canon Cary-Elwes, himself a fine musician, played a prominent part. A local Peterborough paper reported very favourably on 'Cary-Elwes Concerts. A Feast of Delicious Music', which were in aid of the loan for the building of All Souls' Schools. An insight into the social concerns at the time is given by the appeal urging support for the St. Ethelbert's free soup kitchen at Slough and the concert held at Costessey in aid of boots for needy children (twenty were equipped).

Fr Dudley Charles Cary-Elwes (seated) and his curate in about 1919

The 1914-18 War and its aftermath had a decisive effect on the country, affecting the national psyche and leading to many social changes. While, of course, the doctrines and core values of Catholics remained unchanged, the social changes, including greater mobility, shifting populations, the economic climate and the changes in the social strata, did affect the way in which the Catholic Church in the Diocese operated. This was the new situation in which Bishop Cary-Elwes had to lead the Diocese.

Universities, Friars, Culture

Universities

Since the early days of Bishops Wareing and Amherst, great efforts had been made to provide schools for elementary education of the Catholic children in the Diocese. Similarly, some seminaries had been established to educate, or at least to train, men for the priesthood. What had been lacking was the opportunity for Catholics to enjoy an education at the universities which, in effect, meant Oxford and Cambridge.

Although the universities had dropped the requirement that undergraduates had to be Anglican, or at least to subscribe to the Thirty-Nine Articles in order to receive a degree, Catholics were still barred from Oxford and Cambridge. They were barred by the Church. The Church authorities feared that the university would be a grave danger to the faith and morals of Catholic students. When, in 1864, one hundred Catholics, mainly laymen, signed a petition to the Hierarchy urging that a Catholic Hall be established at Oxford, the Bishops rejected the proposal. Bishop Riddell, who was concerned chiefly about Cambridge which was in his Diocese, was forthright. He said, *'We cannot be called upon to give money to help aristocrats and snobs on the high road to Hell'.*

In the eighteen-eighties, however, some Bishops were allowing a small number of Catholics, by way of exception, to attend Oxford or Cambridge. The nephew of the Duke of Norfolk, for example, was one such exception.

The pressure for admission continued and it was led from Cambridge by academics such as Anatole von Hugel. In 1894, Cardinal Vaughan received a petition urging the Hierarchy to ask Rome to lift the ban. The petition contained four hundred and thirty-six signatures including those of almost eighty graduate priests. Canon Scott, parish priest of Our Lady and the English Martyrs in Cambridge, added his testimony, saying that none of the Catholics who had already attended the universities had lost their faith. It was argued that, because of the changed conditions, the universities no longer posed a threat to the Faith. Rome was petitioned and, with uncharacteristic promptness, responded favourably in 1895. One condition, in addition to the stipulation that the undergraduates should have lectures provided on Catholic doctrine, philosophy and history, was that a Catholic chaplain should be appointed.

Canon Christopher Scott, D.D. V.G., Rector 1883-1922

Canon Scott's view was that a separate university chaplaincy was unnecessary, since the undergraduates' spiritual needs could be adequately catered for at his large parish church. Nevertheless, a succession of chaplains was appointed one of whom, Fr Marshall, later became a Canon and Vicar General of Northampton Diocese and parish priest at Ely. The longest serving chaplain was Mgr Alfred Gilbey. He was chaplain for one hundred terms from 1932 to 1965. His evident holiness and civilizing influence commended him to the University and to the Diocese. He was renowned for the very great number of converts he received into the Church and also for the very many priestly vocations he fostered. A notable convert who came by way of the chaplaincy, but at an earlier time, was Charles Grant who was then aged fourteen and who later became a priest and then Bishop of Northampton.

The Chaplain was not, strictly speaking, a diocesan matter or appointment, but the Bishop of Northampton, with the Archbishop of Birmingham, was a key figure in the Universities (later the Oxford and Cambridge) Catholic Education Board that had responsibility for the chaplaincy. Certainly, the Cambridge Chaplaincy had a great effect on the life of the Diocese. Many priests in the Diocese were, and are, graduates of Cambridge and many of these had their priestly vocations aroused and fostered at the Catholic Chaplaincy.

Friars

It was noted how, in the mediaeval period, the Friars were prominently connected with the university and how, in our Diocese at Cambridge, this was especially true of the Franciscans.

Monsignor Alfred Gilbey

Franciscans

In the post-Restoration period, the Franciscans were again a significant part of the Diocesan landscape, both at Cambridge and elsewhere. The Franciscans first arrived in the Diocese in 1894, when they established a junior Seminary at Buckingham, providing training for aspirants for the Order. In 1947, at the suggestion of Bishop Parker, the College changed to become an independent, fee-paying boarding school and the Friars also set up the parish in Buckingham with many out-stations for Mass.

In 1946, the Franciscans moved their house of studies from Forest Gate to East Bergholt, where the young Friars Minor and their Conventual brethren (who had a parish in Northampton) were trained for the priesthood. The Friars also went out from this centre to care for the parish of Brantham, work as chaplains to a hospital and do regular parish supply work in the Diocese. They were particularly involved in ecumenical work locally and gave a significant theological input into the Diocese, for which Fr Eric Doyle O.F.M. was particularly noteworthy.

Student Friars at East Bergholt

As for Cambridge, the Franciscans returned there in the late nineteen-thirties and many of them studied at the University. Their house, St. Bonaventure's, became a centre for the work of caring for immigrants, with Fr Benignus O.F.M. being chairman of the Racial Integration Society. One Franciscan priest there was an Assistant Chaplain at the University.

Dominicans

The Domincans came back to the Diocese in the period between the Wars and have had an influence that goes far beyond what might have been expected from the relatively small number of Friars.

Dominicans at Thrapston

In 1924, they opened their school for boys at Laxton in Northamptonshire, which was based on a distinctively humane and Christian philosophy of education that was most cogently set out by Fr Gerald Vann O.P. Several of the Friars at the school contributed to the Catholic life of the Diocese in a variety of ways. As we would expect from Dominicans, they frequently supplied preachers, but additionally they helped the ongoing formation of the Diocesan Clergy with study days and conferences on theology and liturgy. One recalls particularly Fr Sebastian Bullough O.P., who taught Scripture, and Fr Gerard Meath O.P. The history of Thrapston parish is interesting in this context. In 1940, a Dominican spent a week's holiday cycling round the villages on the border of Northamptonshire and Huntingdonshire in search of Catholics. He discovered thirty-seven children who had no means of getting to Mass. This led to the opening of a Mass centre at Thrapston in the Girl Guide hall and, for five years, a Dominican from Laxton did a fifty mile journey every Sunday to say Mass for the Catholics there.

Gerald Vann

Kenelm Foster

The Dominicans' other house in the Diocese was Blackfriars St Michael's at Cambridge, which they set up in 1938. This was not a house for their students, nor primarily a parish. Fr Aidan Nichols O.P. says that it could best be described as a 'house of writers'. Certainly, the Dominicans there had close links with the University. Fr Kenelm Foster O.P. was for many years a Lecturer and then Reader in Italian in the University and was an acknowledged authority on Dante. In his later years, Fr Sebastian Bullough O.P. taught Hebrew and Syriac in the University's department of Semitic languages. At various times, including the present, Dominicans have been chaplains for Catholic undergraduates at Cambridge.

Sebastian Bullough

Culture

In this period of the nineteen twenties and thirties, there was a renewal of a certain Catholic culture in England. Much of this was initiated, or was fostered, by a number of outstanding Dominicans among others. But it was spread more widely through the works of certain lay people.

One of those who had a far reaching effect was G.K.Chesterton and he had been received into the Catholic Church at Beaconsfield and lived and worked there. Not far from there, at Pigotts in Buckinghamshire, was Eric Gill and his family and a small colony of Catholic artists, sculptors and stained-glass workers who were influential members of this Catholic cultural renewal. It was Eric Gill who designed the Catholic church at Gorleston, which exemplifies the ideas and attitudes of this culture.

Walsingham

Although the Shrine at Walsingham had been suppressed at the Reformation, the memory of it lingered on in the Catholic consciousness. While the site was in non-Catholic hands and while there were no Catholics in Walsingham, the best that could be done was to erect a shrine to Our Lady of Walsingham in the church at King's Lynn.

But devotion to Our Lady did return to Walsingham and the restoration of a shrine there in 1934 was a moment of supreme joy for Bishop Youens. The shrine could not be revived at its original site, but it could be, and was, established in the Slipper Chapel. Since the suppression of the Shrine at the time of Henry VIII, the Slipper Chapel had fallen into decay and over the years had been used as a blacksmith's forge and then as some sort of stable by a farmer. A cottage had been added at the East end. There appears to have been three chimney stacks and another cottage was up against one wall.

The Slipper Chapel as it was when bought in 1894

In 1894, Charlotte Boyd, who had been a member of an Anglican Sisterhood, bought this property and, in the same year, was received into the Catholic Church. Charlotte Boyd had the place renovated and the cottages removed so that it could become once again a Chapel and a Shrine. She gave the place to the Benedictines of Downside Abbey who later transferred it to the Bishop of Northampton. And so, in 1934, Bishop Youens led thousands, headed by nine Bishops, several Abbots and Cardinal Bourne in the first National Pilgrimage to the restored National Shrine of Our Lady of Walsingham.

There has been a constant stream of pilgrims there ever since. In May 1945, after the Italian armistice, Bishop Parker offered Mass with American troops in the 'Old Place' - the Priory ruins. When war seemed to threaten again in 1948, there was a great National Pilgrimage for Peace, part of a nationwide crusade for peace. Fourteen groups of thirty men, each group carrying a heavy cross, walked for a fortnight from various parts of England to Walsingham. They came from as far north as Middlesbrough and as far south as Canterbury. The crosses were set up in the field beyond the Slipper Chapel as the fourteen Stations of the Cross. In the Marian Year 1954, Archbishop Gerald O'Hara, the Apostolic Delegate, crowned the statue of Our Lady with a crown of 18ct. gold embellished with 118 precious stones, which had been sent by people from all parts, even as far away as Chicago. It was said that, in the name of the Holy Father, the Delegate *'restored to the brow of our National Madonna the crown filched from her brow by Henry VIII'.*

The Cross-carrying pilgrims leave the Stations of the Cross at Walsingham, 2 July, 1948

World War II

Before the Diocese could reach and celebrate its centenary, the Second World War broke out in September 1939. Two months later, on 14 November 1939, Bishop Youens died and the Diocese was left leaderless for fifteen months.

On 8 December 1940, Leo Parker received from the Apostolic Delegation the news of his appointment as Bishop of Northampton and instructions to send his acceptance in cypher to Lisbon, from whence it would be forwarded to Rome. He was consecrated at the Cathedral on 11 February 1941, a bitterly cold winter's day. Food and petrol were rationed, maps were almost unobtainable, signposts were rare and there was constant fear of enemy bombing. Obviously, being a Bishop was not going to be easy, but Bishop Parker at once set to and served the Diocese valiantly for the next twenty-six years. We may look at the struggles and achievements of his Episcopate later.

Bishop Leo Parker

Taking Stock After One Hundred Years

For the moment, Bishop Parker was aware of the approaching Centenary and, like Bishop Wareing before him, he doubtless looked back to see what he had inherited in this Northampton Diocese. For the centenary in 1950, a 'Centenary Souvenir' booklet was produced detailing the history and fortunes of the Diocese since the Restoration of the Hierarchy. It might be useful and interesting for us now to review a summary of that record.

Northamptonshire

NORTHAMPTON

In 1864, there were in Northampton about 1,000 to 1,200 Catholics. A day school had been started in a large room in King Street and, in 1851, was moved to Woolmonger Road. The Notre Dame Convent started in Abington Street in 1870 and, in 1873, St. Mary's School was opened on the Mounts. The Sisters of Nazareth moved to their new house next to the Cathedral in 1873. Bishop Amherst bought the extant portion of the mediaeval hospital of St. John's in Bridge Street to be used as a chapel. (It was later sold in the nineteen-nineties.)

In 1880, it was estimated that out of the town population of 57,553, there were 1,000 Catholics and in that same year land was bought for a boys' school in Clare Street.

During the Second World War, it became clear that there was a need to expand the Catholic parish because of the increased number of Catholics - evacuees, British, American and Allied military - who had come into the town and the county.

The Jesus and Mary Sisters were here for a short time and the Sisters of the Sacred Heart from Homerton stayed at Bishop's House and taught in The Mounts. The Notre Dame School from Willesden came to join the Notre Dame School in Abington Street.

BUGBROOKE was a Catholic Mass centre and Mass was celebrated in ABINGTON to cater for the evacuees. At first, Mass was in the Anglican hall and then, in 1946, Fr Eric Phillips took up residence in Ashburnham Road and later in Park Avenue North. On 1 May 1947, the temporary church of St. Gregory was opened there. There were weekly Mass centres at DUSTON and MOULTON and Mass was said occasionally at Berrywood, St. Crispin's Hospital, St. Andrew's Hospital and at Creaton Sanatorium.

Evacuees

BOUGHTON had various occupants - an army unit, then Italian prisoners, then German prisoners of war and finally European Volunteer Workers. Bishop Parker's Pastoral Letters appeared in German, Latvian and Polish, and Mass was said there by chaplains of a variety of nationalities.

The Polish Sisters of the Holy Family of Nazareth opened a school for Polish girls at **PITSFORD HALL**, and at **OXENDEN** the Missionaries of St. Francis de Sales had a boarding school and provided two public Masses on Sundays.

Convent of Polish Sisters of the Holy Family of Nazareth

TOWCESTER had a temporary chapel of St. George in 1949.

There was a Catholic bookshop in **NORTHAMPTON** in Langham Place; a Men's Club in part of the old Seminary of St.Felix; and a Youth Club which moved from a Catholic shop premises to the old canteen in the Arcade and finally to the stable block at the back of Cathedral House.

In 1950, in **NORTHAMPTON** the schools were full and in the previous year there had been 219 baptisms including 31 converts.

PETERBOROUGH

For eight years, Mass was said in a room, until the chapel of the Holy Family was opened in 1856 in Queen Street. The funds for this were collected by Fr Seed in Ireland. In 1880, out of a population of 25,000, only 150 were Catholics. The Sisters of St. Vincent de Paul opened a school in 1893. Three years later, the church of St. Peter in Chains and All Souls was opened. It was reopened in 1904 after two bays had been added. A former parish priest, Fr Cary-Elwes, was commemorated in 1934 by the new hall. In 1949, a temporary church of St. Oswald was erected at Walton. There were Mass centres at SIBSON, CONINGTON and YAXLEY and occasional Masses at WHITTLESEY and THORNEY. Peterborough served OUNDLE until 1939.

The Sisters of Charity of St.Vincent de Paul

ASTON-LE-WALLS continued with a church and day school. It had a new elementary school in 1927.

In 1912, a small church of St. Joseph was built at WOODFORD HALSE, which was served from Aston-le-Walls.

At **WEEDON** in 1851, a wooden chapel of Our Lady of Victories was opened and at first served from Northampton. In 1880, Fr

Catholic Church, Aston-le-Walls

Jenks House

Church of Our Lady of the Sacred Heart, Wellingborough

Keane lived there for a short time and the population was 2000, of whom 51 were Catholics, plus 110 military with their wives and children. During the Second World War, a Mill Hill Missioner lived there.

OUNDLE was a Mass centre served from Peterborough until the Jenks family gave up their house in 1894. At that time there were no more than 10 Catholics in the town. The Belgian refugees brought the Mass back there between October 1914 and May 1919. In 1924, the Dominicans from Laxton reopened the Oundle Mission and then the clergy from Peterborough took over. Mass was said in the old Town Hall. On 8 August 1948, Bishop Parker opened a chapel dedicated to St. Wilfrid in a disused Baptist chapel.

THRAPSTON had a temporary church opened in January 1949 and in that same year Apethorpe Hall was set up via the Home Office as an Approved School for Boys, dedicated to St. John Bosco.

WELLINGBOROUGH, in 1869, was served from Northampton with Mass on a weekday for four families. From 1870, two rooms were rented for Mass and then, in 1881, Fr Bernard Murray went to live there. At that time the population was 13,000, of whom 139 were Catholics. There were 13 Baptisms in 1880 of whom 10 were converts. The church of Our Lady of the Sacred Heart was built in Ranelagh Road with an adjoining house and elementary school.

At **HARROWDEN**, there was the church of St. Hubert since 1905, with a mortuary chapel to the memory of Lord Vaux.

Mr Cary-Elwes, the Squire of **GREAT BILLING** and the father of the future Bishop, was converted with his family to the Catholic Church. He was permitted to have a private oratory, which later became public. It was served from Northampton with two Masses in the week. The first resident priest, Fr Blackman, arrived in 1876 and, three years later, the church of Our Lady of Perpetual Succour was built by Mr Cary-Elwes. There were 80 Catholics in the village at that time, many of them converts. The Notre Dame Sisters opened a rest home in the village and, during World War II, Great Billing served SYWELL Airfield and CASTLE ASHBY.

Billing Church

DAVENTRY had its first resident priest in 1880 and a room in the presbytery was used for Mass. At his own expense, Lord Braye enlarged some stables at the back of his property and converted them into a chapel of St. Mark, which was opened in 1882. At that time, of the 4,000 people in the town, just 55 were Catholics. In 1916, the church of Our Lady of Charity and St. Augustine was opened and, in 1950, Daventry served WEEDON and LONG BUCKBY.

The Duchess of Buccleuch, a convert, is regarded as the foundress of the **KETTERING** Mission. In 1891, the people there begged the Bishop for a priest and he sent Fr Stanley from Newmarket. At first, Mass was said in the billiard room in Tirrell's Temperance Hotel and then in a room rented in Loasby and Miller's shoe factory. When the presbytery was completed in 1892, the ground floor served as a chapel until the temporary church was ready. In 1893, Bishop Riddell offered Pontifical Mass in the chapel. In 1924, Fr Lockyer came as resident priest and in 1937 an assistant priest came. Fr Charles Grant, later to become Bishop, came in October 1940, when the new church of St. Edward the Confessor was opened. Fr Grant remained there until 1945 and in the following year Bishop Parker consecrated the church. A community of Franciscan nuns had been there for a time, but in 1937 they were replaced by Ursulines, who had a High School for girls and a kindergarten.

New Church of St. Edward, Kettering

New Church of Our Lady of Walsingham, Corby

RUSHDEN was a daughter mission of Wellingborough. A priest's house was built in 1899 and, in 1904, a church was partly built. In 1936, a hall was used as a temporary church. The Griffin family had an oratory open to the public, but it ceased when they left the district.

CORBY and the country round it was a Catholic stronghold in Elizabethan times, but this had been extinguished in the Penal period. Mass returned in the twentieth century to BRIGSTOCK Manor. Some time before 1924, Canon Tonks of Kettering offered Mass in a cottage in Corby village. The great industrial development in Corby of the Stewart and Lloyd steel works brought many Catholic families from Scotland. The church of Our Lady of Walsingham was opened and the Holy Cross Sisters had an infant school there. Thrapston became a daughter mission of Corby. In 1949, Mass began to be offered occasionally at Weldon Industrial Hostel and again at Brigstock. Mass was said at Pottersbury Lodge, in the extreme South of the county, in the home of George Beale and was served from Wolverton.

Bedfordshire

SHEFFORD, in 1850, was the only Mass centre in the county. In 1868, Fr Collis opened the Diocesan Orphanage, dedicated to St Francis. Because of the wartime conditions, Bishop Parker formed a Diocesan Catholic Child Rescue and Welfare Society, in 1943, to include babies of two weeks old. They were cared for by the Bon Secours nuns. The society then extended to their Home in Sheringham in 1945.

Bishop Riddell set up the Diocesan Seminary at 23 High Street. (It was closed in 1908.)

There were few Catholics there in the nineteenth century - at one time there were only 8 at Mass. In 1880, out of a population of 1100, the Catholics numbered 153. The church of St. Francis was built in 1884 and the old chapel became the sacristy. Shefford served Arlesey.

BIGGLESWADE was a foundation from Shefford in 1905 and, in 1920, its church of St. Peter was opened and at first it was served by the Assumptionists from Hitchin.

A typical Iron Church

Church of St. Peter, Marlow

Church of St. Ethelbert, Slough

BEDFORD. Elizabeth Vine of Bedford was baptised at Shefford on 5 May 1834, but otherwise Bedford has no recorded Catholic history until 1863. Fr Warmoll came then to say Mass on Christmas Eve in 'a wash-house near the prison, the last little house on the left of Gore Place'. In 1867, he built a small house, part of which served as a school and, in 1874, the chancel end of a church was built. The church was completed in 1912. The Daughters of the Holy Ghost opened a school for girls in Bromham Road. By 1950, there was a temporary chapel at KEMPSTON. A church was built at AMPTHILL in 1935 and FLITWICK was also served from there.

LUTON. A mission was started in 1845, but abandoned after two years. In the eighteen-eighties, with 160 Catholics, Luton came under Bedford. In 1884, the first resident priest, Fr J.O'Connor, said Mass in his house. Soon after this, an iron church was erected in Castle Street. In 1939, there was a temporary church of St. Joseph in Gardenia Avenue and, in 1946, a Mission was started at STOPSLEY.

DUNSTABLE was entrusted to the Congregation of St. Vincent de Paul and, in 1927, the church of the Immaculate Virgin was built. At TODDINGTON, a domestic chapel was open to local Catholics.

LEIGHTON BUZZARD. In 1892, Fr Parkes offered Mass monthly in a hired room and, in 1895, the first resident priest, Fr C. O'Reilly, arrived. Two years later, an iron church was erected in Beaudesert Road. The number of Catholics was estimated to be 40 in 1939. During the Second World War, the Catholic population was greatly increased and several chaplains of various nationalities visited their people, who were in a number of hostels. Mass was also offered at the R.A.F. camp at CRANFIELD and at HARROLD.

Buckinghamshire

The Mission at **MARLOW** was founded in 1844 and so pre-dates the Restoration of the Hierarchy. Charles Scott-Murray, who had become a Catholic under the influence of Newman, rented a cottage and installed Fr Peter Coop to say Mass there. In July 1846, the church of St. Peter was opened. It was designed by A.W. Pugin and was the first public Catholic church to be built in the county since the Reformation. The Redemptorists served the parish from 1848 to 1851. In 1856, the Sisters of Charity had a school in Marlow.

OLNEY. Mass was first said here in 1899 in the house of Mr Glasspole. A church was opened in 1900 and the Daughters of the Holy Ghost had a convent school there from 1902. HARROLD was served from Olney in 1946.

SLOUGH had a chapel of St. James in the school in Baylis House from 1830 to 1907. The house had been designed by Wren and built for Dr Godolphin, the Provost of Eton. In 1885, there were only 82 Catholics in the Slough Mission and in that year a warehouse was converted into a temporary church. In the next year, part of this was altered and opened as a school, while another part became a soup kitchen. In eighteen-ninety, 37,881 meals were served to the poor. On one day, free dinner was given to 482 poor children of all denominations and later, to 300 adults. The Bernardine nuns established a High School for Girls in 1897. The parish school had been built in 1894 at the expense of the Duchess of Bucchleuch. At the Christmas Midnight Mass in 1907, Fr Clemente announced that the Lady Superior of the Bernardines would build a church in memory of her parents. This church, St. Ethelbert's, was consecrated on 19 April 1910. Its style was based on that of churches of East Anglia, particularly the one at Wells, Norfolk. In 1919, a temporary Mass centre was established at SALT HILL. At FARNHAM ROYAL a junior school was built in 1939 and Fr Houghton was the first rector of St. Anthony's church there in 1943. A Mass centre was started at IVER in the following year.

BURNHAM had Mass for the Belgian refugees during the First World War and then, in 1935, a temporary church of Our Lady of Peace and St. Laurence was built. It was extended in 1943.

ETON was a daughter Mission from Slough. In 1914, Lord Braye built a church to serve as the parish church for Eton and Datchet and also for for the Catholic boys at Eton College. Dedicated to Our Lady of Sorrows, it was built in reparation to the Mother of God, in whose honour Eton had been founded. In 1950, it was served by the Canons Regular of the Lateran in Datchet. In DATCHET, they built the church of St. Augustine and, in 1950, they had a Secondary School for boys.

Chapel of the Mother of God "Cruci Adstanti", Eton

Chapel of Our Lady, Eton

CHESHAM BOIS was cared for by the Carmelites in 1908, having converted a disused railway hut into a chapel. Two years later, they had the use of a second-hand iron building. This was replaced by a permanent church of Our Lady of Perpetual Succour in 1915. The Poor Servants of the Mother of God had a convent and school there and there was a Mass centre at CHESHAM.

GERRARDS CROSS. The Carmelites moved here from Chesham Bois and, in 1915, built the church of St. Joseph. In 1928, the Holy Cross Sisters took over the historic Grange Hotel for a convent and day school and, in 1930, the Brigettine Sisters opened a convent and a chapel of St. Richard and the English Martyrs at IVER HEATH. Gerrards Cross served CHALFONT ST. GILES, DENHAM and LATIMER.

HIGH WYCOMBE was originally cared for by priests from Marlow. Then Sir Philip Rose of Rayners agreed to share the services of a priest who should be his chaplain and who would live at High Wycombe. Mass was first said there on 3 December 1889 at 17 High Street. In 1894, the church of St. Augustine was opened. The congregation of The Daughters of Jesus took over a convent and school for boys and girls from the Bernardines.

Convent at High Wycombe

Interesting correspondence of the time

Beaconsfield Chapel, 1927

BEACONSFIELD was a daughter Mission from High Wycombe and was founded in 1920. Mass was said in the Railway Hotel. It was here that G.K.Chesterton was received into the church and made his first Holy Communion. In 1927, the permanent church of St. Teresa was begun and later it was enlarged as a memorial to Chesterton. The Bon Secours Sisters set up a convent and hospital in the town. Chesterton's house, 'Top Meadow', became a Catholic centre and later housed the work of the Converts' Aid Society.

Above: Princes Risborough, Whit Sunday 1928

PRINCES RISBOROUGH. The Mission was first served in 1922 from High Wycombe and then by the Jesuits from Heythrop in 1926. The first chapel of Our Lady of Lourdes was at the Chalfont Hall on the Aylesbury Road. In 1928, there was a chapel in Longwick Road. Fr F. Dreeves M.H.M. was the first resident priest in 1936 and, in the next year, he built the permanent church of St. Teresa of the Child Jesus, which was consecrated in 1945. The Daughters of Jesus established a convent and a juniorate for candidates for their Order. When they later left, this became a private school. A Sunday Mass was supplied in the old surgery at Great Missenden.

AYLESBURY. In 1843, there was an abortive attempt to start a Mission when the Earl of Shrewsbury gave money for altar furniture. There were plans for a church to be designed by A.W. Pugin in 1851, but six years later the Mission was closed. Mass was occasionally offered in the house of Mr Casey and then in that of Mr Roche. In 1880, there were 30 Catholics out of a population of 28,899. A resident priest arrived in December 1888 and celebrated Mass in his house until 1892. Then, in that year, a temporary iron church was erected. The church of St. Joseph was built in 1927 and the convent of St. Louis established a school. In 1949, the parish hall was opened and Sunday Mass was offered at the Chapel of St. Edmund, Stoke Mandeville hospital, the Womens' Prison and at Wendover.

BUCKINGHAM. The first Mass here was offered in a cottage in Elm Street by Fr Thaddeus Hermans O.F.M. He then took a house in West Street. In 1895, St. Bernadine's College was built and a large room in the college was used as a chapel until a church could be built. The church was opened in 1912 and consecrated in 1937. At first, the college was for students of the Order. Then it became a Grammar School. The Franciscans had a Mass centre at FARTHINGHOE, where Mrs Rush made her garden-house into a chapel of Our Lady of the Fields and she paid for a bus to collect the Catholics from BRACKLEY. When she died in 1940, her chapel was given up, but Mass was started at Brackley, where Mrs Meredith provided a store room, converted into a chapel, until she left in 1948. Then Mass was offered in the Women's Institute. The chapel of St. Alban was opened in WINSLOW HALL in 1948 and Buckingham served a camp chapel at WHITFIELD and at TOWCESTER. The Franciscan Sisters of the Divine Motherhood had a house at Buckingham.

WOLVERTON. The opening of the L.N.W. Railway Carriage Works in the eighteen-sixties led to an increased need for Mass. The Mission was an offshoot from Aylesbury, although it was served from Northampton. The first Mass there was on 23 July 1865 and the church of St. Francis de Sales was opened in June 1867. There was a resident priest and, by 1880, there were 90 Catholics.

BLETCHLEY. Mass was offered here from 1912 and, in 1920, the chapel of St. Thomas Aquinas was opened. From 1930, it came under the care of Woburn Sands.

WOBURN SANDS. For some years after 1926 it was served from Bedford and the original Mass centre was the club room of the Fir Tree Hotel. In 1931, the temporary church of Our Lady of Perpetual Succour was opened.

THORNTON COLLEGE. The convent of Jesus and Mary and boarding school provided a place for Sunday Mass for local Catholics.

Cambridgeshire

CAMBRIDGE. In 1887, Mrs Lyne Stephens gave a house for the priest and she offered to pay for a new church. The foundation stone was laid on 30 June 1887 and the church was consecrated in 1890 and dedicated to Our Lady and the English Martyrs. There was a parish school.

ST. EDMUND'S HOUSE - a house of studies for Secular Clergy was provided by the Duke of Norfolk and a new chapel was built there in 1916. FISHER HOUSE, with its oratory of Corpus Christi, was the Catholic Chaplaincy for Undergraduates. The Religious Orders with houses in Cambridge in 1950 were - Franciscans, Dominicans, Benedictines, De La Salle Brothers, Canonesses of St. Augustine, the Fathers of Charity, Sisters of Hope Nursing Home, and the Institute of the Blessed Virgin Mary. There was a Mass centre at ABINGDON until 1949 in the Bretherton household and at LINTON, SHELFORD and SAWSTON. In 1947, a temporary wooden church of St. Laurence was erected at CHESTERTON and there was a Mass centre at HISTON in the Manor House. The Carmelite Nuns had a convent at WATERBEACH from 1937 and at BOTTISHAM there was a Polish school for boys with two resident priests.

The completed church in 1890 - Our Lady and the English Martyrs, Cambridge

WISBECH had a Mass centre from 1840 and a resident priest in 1852. Two years later, the church of St. Mary and St. Charles was opened. The Sisters of Providence (Rosminian) opened St. Audrey's convent and school in 1928 and, ten years later, a parish day school was started. A large number of Irish landworkers settled at WISBECH FEN and a priest came from Peterborough to say Mass for them, until Fr Fox came to Wisbech. In 1862, Fr Colpman converted a barn into a chapel at THORNEY TOLL, which was replaced by temporary wood and iron church of St. Patrick, brought over from Ely. Mass was said for workers who came annually for the harvest.

Wisbech Chapel

ELY. Mass was said in the house of Mrs Fischer at Forehill by a priest from Newmarket. In 1890, a resident priest said Mass in his lodgings and, within eighteen months, he had opened an iron church. In 1903, St Ethelreda's church was built. There were Mass centres at LITTLEPORT, SOHAM and SUTTON.

MARCH had an occasional Mass during 1909 and 1910. The Motor Chapel of the Catholic Missionary Society visited there and regular Sunday Mass began. A resident priest came in 1912 and a temporary church of Our Lady of Good Counsel was built. During the Second World War, the Montfort Missionaries served March and Ramsey.

Huntingdonshire

RAMSEY Mission was opened in 1863, with the church of the Sacred Heart and, in 1872, a Mass centre was opened at Huntingdon. In 1876, the priest went to Huntingdon and Ramsey was served from there.

HUNTINGDON had an iron church built on a site which had been bought by cattle dealers. The new church of St. Michael was opened in 1900.

ST. NEOTS was a daughter Mission of Huntingdon. A disused Baptist chapel became a Catholic church of St Joseph, because the Baptists wanted *'to prevent it becoming a cinema'*.

ST. IVES. A convert, Mr George Pauling, bought a plot of land with a wooden hall on it in 1900. This was then used as a chapel. He bought another plot and paid for the removal to there of the old Pugin church of St. Andrew from Cambridge. In 1902, this church was re-erected there. At Hemingford Grey, in St. Ives parish, the Ramsgate Benedictines had a boarding school, which was evacuated there from Ramsgate in World War II.

St. John the Baptist's, Norwich

Norfolk

The tempo of increase in Catholic life in Norfolk and Suffolk was different from that in the rest of the Diocese.

NORWICH, in 1850, had 1,000 Catholics in the two parishes of St. John's and The Holy Apostles. The Sisters of Notre Dame set up a large day school and a boarding school in 1860. The Duke of Norfolk bought the site of the Norwich prison in 1881 and, in 1884, the foundation stone of the new church was laid. The nave, aisles, baptistry and memorial chapel were opened in 1894 and the completed church was inaugurated and blessed by Bishop Keating in 1910. The Jesuits gave up their church in Willow Lane and it became a school. A second church was opened at Fishergate in 1896 and a resident priest went there three years later. In 1904, the Little Sisters of the Assumption had a convent. In 1934, the chapel of Christ the King was opened at Lakenham and there was a Mass centre at Mile Cross.

COSTESSEY, in 1850, had two churches in use, St. Walstan's in the village and the chapel in The Hall. Lack of employment decreased the number of Catholics. In 1868, there was a congregation of 305. From 1872, only the chapel in the Hall was used for the congregation and St. Walstan's was used only for funerals. In 1910, St. Walstan's was reopened as the parochial church and in 1920 the Hall, including its chapel, was demolished. The Sisters of Charity of St. Paul came to look after the school from 1868 to 1872 and then returned again in 1874.

Costessey Old Hall, showing St. Augustine's Chapel

WROXHAM was the home of the Trafford family and the Mission began there in 1869 with the priest living at the Hall and Mass was said in the chapel in the Hall. In 1880, the iron church of St. Michael and St. Helen was built and was served from Norwich.

MASS CENTRES FROM NORWICH. In 1913, there were five Mass centres - NORTH WALSHAM, AYLSHAM, DISS, EAST HARLING and WYMONDHAM. Although these were distant from Norwich, they were easily accessible by train. There was a Mass centre at STOKE in the Hall, the residence of Mr Birkbeck. This was transferred in 1949 to PORINGLAND.

GREAT YARMOUTH, in 1850, had its chapel and cemetery. The Jesuits were in charge of it. In 1947, a Mass centre was established at HEMSBY and, in 1948, a Mass centre was established at the cemetery chapel on the Caister Road. The St. Louis nuns had a Primary and a High School. LOWESTOFT, and GORLESTON were offshoots from Yarmouth.

CROMER was a daughter mission of Norwich. Mass was said in the Red Lion Hotel by priests from Norwich during the summer months, from 1892 to 1894. The church of Our Lady of Refuge was built and opened in 1896 and the presbytery was added in 1904.

Church of St. Mary, Great Yarmouth

SHERINGHAM had a Mission from Cromer. In 1908, part of the church was opened and, two years later, there was a resident priest and then the church was completed. The Bon Secours Sisters had their convent of St. Joseph and the Diocesan Catholic Residential Nursery there.

St. Joseph's Diocesan Nursery of the Catholic Child Protection and Welfare Society, Sheringham

NORTH WALSHAM had a Mass centre served from Sheringham in 1912. The chapel was in Mr Loads' shop. In 1925, a resident priest came and, in 1935, the permanent church of the Sacred Heart was built. On the death of Mr Loads in 1947, his house became the presbytery.

AYLSHAM had Mass twice a month from Norwich. In 1899, the chapel of St. John of the Cross was built by three convert sisters in the grounds of their house, in memory of their brother, S.M. Shepherd, who for forty years had been the Anglican Vicar of Calthorpe in Norfolk.

KING'S LYNN was a Missionary centre and its priests occasionally supplied Costessey and Thetford. It had schools from an early date. In 1897, the church was completely dismantled and rebuilt on a new site. The church has a side chapel reminiscent of the Holy House of Loretto. The statue of Our Lady there was the one blessed by Pope Leo XIII and which became the shrine for the devotion to Our Lady of Walsingham.

WALSINGHAM. In 1930, the Benedictines gave the restored Slipper Chapel to the Bishop of Northampton. In 1935, the Capuchins moved there and had a house-chapel of St. Aelred. They left in 1948. In 1950, a temporary church was opened in Friday Market in the village.

FAKENHAM. In 1905, a priest was sent there to serve the large area around Fakenham. At first, Mass was said in rooms, in shops and private houses. In 1909, a small chapel was built and was designed to be able to be used later as the sacristy to a larger church. In 1946, this was enlarged. There were Mass centres from here at Wells-next-the-Sea, Walsingham and Dereham.

WELLS-NEXT-THE-SEA. There is mention in 1897 of six Catholics here. In 1928, there is the church of Our Lady Star of the Sea, but no resident priest.

HUNSTANTON. A chapel was built here in 1904 - Our Lady of Perpetual Succour and St. Edmund, King and Martyr. Mass was supplied from here to Dersingham and Bincham Newton.

SWAFFHAM was the most ancient Mission in Norfolk, after Norwich. The Jesuits were there from 1682 to 1730. In 1914, the Daughters of Divine Charity had a school there. The Catholic Missionary Society visited the town in 1908 and were responsible for the Mission. For many years, Mass was offered in Swaffham Theatre. In 1922, a temporary church was erected.

DOWNHAM MARKET. Here a Catholic lady began a private 'Catholic Home for Afflicted Children'. The first resident priest came in 1937. The church of St. Dominic was blessed in 1941.

OXBURGH was one of the oldest Missions in Norfolk. In 1850, it already had a church and school. The church was dedicated to the Immaculate Conception and St. Margaret. The Bedingfield family was still the great support it had been since 1480.

St. Stephen's Church, Lynford

THETFORD was an 'old Border Mission'. In 1850, it had a church, school and presbytery. In 1879, Mrs Lyne Stephens erected a new school to replace the old schoolroom. With a certified teacher, it got a government grant, but this ceased in the nineteen-thirties. During the Second World War, the Christian Brothers housed St. Gilbert's Approved School for junior boys in the Forest.

LYNFORD. In the forest was the church of Our Lady of Consolation and St. Stephen. Mrs Lyne Stephens lived there at Lynford Park. She had the church built in 1879. A resident priest came in 1881.

WYMONDHAM. From 1893, there had been the chapel of the Sacred Heart in the house of Mr Newton, which was served from Beccles. This was given up when Mr Newton left in 1904. In 1911, the Motor Mission visited the town and, in the next year, Mass was being said there by priests from Norwich. In 1913, there was Mass on alternate Sundays and, on the other Sundays, there was an evening service. The congregation at these services was about forty, of whom about ten were Catholics. Several converts were made. There was a chapel in the grounds of Arthur Glasspoole and, in 1926, there was a resident priest. A temporary church of Our Lady and St. Thomas of Canterbury was opened in 1938. Later, Fr Cowin built a permanent church as a memorial for the Prisoners of War under the Japanese.

Our Lady and St. Thomas of Canterbury - a memorial for the Prisoners of War under the Japanese

EAST DEREHAM. In 1834, there is a record of a few Catholics here. In 1911, the Motor Mission gave a series of lectures in the Corn Hall, which were attended by over 700 people each night. Mass was offered at intervals in private houses. In 1925, the Guild of Ransom presented a temporary church of the Sacred Heart and Margaret Mary.

East Dereham

DISS. The French Ursulines spent four years at Diss up to 1911. Then the district was entrusted to St. John's, Norwich, and Mass was offered monthly until 1937. The Travelling Mission revived the Mass centre in 1948 and, in 1950, Mass was being said in Wren's café and the centre was under the care of the chaplain to the Carmelites at Quidenham. He also offered Mass at the Polish camp in Buckenham. SCOLE LODGE was a convent during the Second World War and from it six Sunday Masses were celebrated in the neighbourhood.

QUIDENHAM was the home of the Albermarles and there were occasional Masses in their domestic chapel. In 1948, they gave the house to the Carmelite nuns who had come from Rushmere. Sunday Mass was open to the people.

EAST HARLING was a Mass centre served from Norwich. Every Thursday, Mass was said in the 'Women's Inebriate Home'. East Harling was a Catholic centre in Penal times.

GILLINGHAM was served from Beccles. In 1898, a church was built by George Kenyon who, after his conversion, served as a Papal Zouave and, while fighting for the Pope in 1870 at Porta Pia, was taken prisoner in Penoa.

Suffolk

IPSWICH. By 1850, there was already a commodious chapel. In 1860, Bishop Riddell invited the Sisters of Jesus and Mary from Lyons. They set up a house and orphanage. In 1862, a mob attacked the convent and the presbytery. The sisters, in secular dress, went to a new convent. In 1892, the Sisters built an elementary school. Another church was built in

Church of St. Felix, Felixstowe

1861, dedicated to St. Pancras. The Carmelites had been here at Rushmere before moving to Quidenham. The De La Salle Brothers had a Secondary School for boys.

FELIXSTOWE was an offshoot from Ipswich. The first resident priest came there in 1899 and, in 1912, the church of St. Felix was built and then enlarged in 1932. The Sisters of Jesus and Mary had a convent and a boarding and day school since 1917.

WOODBRIDGE had a Mass centre in the house of Dr Moore. In 1871, there was a church in Crown Place. In the eighteen-eighties there were just 16 Catholics at Woodbridge, 3 at Framlingham, 8 at Southwold and 1 at Aldburgh. In 1921, a resident priest came there. His successor converted the old Assembly Rooms into a church of St. Thomas of Canterbury, which was opened in 1930. There were Mass centres at Wickham Market and Hollesley Bay Borstal. The Carmelites were at Woodbridge at one time, before they moved to Rushmere.

ALDEBURGH and **LEISTON**. The convent school at THELLUSON LODGE is the start of the Mission at Aldburgh. Mass was said in the convent until 1919, when the nuns returned to France. In 1925, the foundation stone was laid of the church of Our Lady and St. Peter. LEISTON was served from here first in 1911. There was a Mass centre in FRAMLINGHAM (where many martyrs had been in gaol). Mass was said in the Crown Hotel.

SOUTHWOLD. During the eighteen-nineties Mass was celebrated in the house of Mr Crimmon. In 1902, Mass was said in a wooden building which had been a net shed. The Sacred Heart Church was built in 1916 and had been paid for with money from the will of Miss Amy Amor Auld, who had converted and entered the Benedictine Abbey at East Bergholt. During the Second World War, Southwold had a Mass centre at HALESWORTH.

Our Lady Star of the Sea, Lowestoft

LOWESTOFT was a daughter Mission of Yarmouth. In 1867, the Jesuits at Yarmouth hired the Assembly Rooms in Crown Street for Sunday Mass. A net loft was converted into a chapel in 1873 and then Mass was moved to The Armory. There was a resident priest in 1894 and, in 1902, a large brick church of Our Lady of the Sea was opened. The Sisters of the Immaculate Heart of Mary came in 1903 and, in 1921, the Sisters of Mary came to run the boarding and day school at KIRKLEY CLIFF.

GORLESTON ON SEA had a resident priest in 1896 and, in 1889, a chapel had been opened. In 1939, the church of St. Peter, designed by Eric Gill, was opened.

BUNGAY was an offshoot of Flixton. In 1930, a chapel and priest's house was built. The Dowager Duchess of Norfolk presented a school in 1873. A church was partly built in 1889 and completed in 1891 and dedicated to St. Edmund King and Martyr. There was a Mass centre at BROCKDISH. The church was served by the English Benedictines.

St. Peter's, Gorleston

BECCLES was also served by the Benedictines. In 1889, Mass was said in the priest's house. A new chapel was built in 1891 and a later large church was opened in 1901. The completed church of St. Benet was consecrated in 1908. The Poor Servants of the Mother of God had a convent and a preparatory school for boys and girls. There were Mass centres at GILLINGHAM and LODDON. SCOLE and EYE. The Catholic life was maintained when the Notre Dame Convent from Norwich settled at SCOLE during wartime evacuation. The chaplain kept up a regular Mass at EYE.

BURY ST. EDMUNDS. For some time, this was the Jesuit centre - 'College of the Apostles'. In 1837, there was already a large church. The Jesuits continued to minister there until the nineteen-thirties, when the Secular Priests took over. The Sisters of St. Louis had a school there.

Church of St. Edmund Bury St. Edmunds

COLDHAM COTTAGE kept the continuity of the Faith. The Baptism registers go back to the eighteenth century. The priest took over the school. One year, he made stilts, so that the children could get to school through the deep mud. The chapel was transferred to the school building. In 1870, a new church of Our Lady of the Immaculate Conception was formed from the altered priest's house.

NEWMARKET was an offshoot of Cambridge. Mass was first offered in the house of Mr Bocock. The resident priest came in 1857. A church was built in 1863 and then enlarged and dedicated to Our Lady Immaculate and St. Ethelreda in 1874. The district was handed over to the care of the Canons Regular of the Holy Cross in 1876 and then, in 1886, the Secular priests took over. The Sisters of St Louis had a school and convent.

KIRTLING. The Mission was established at Kirtling Towers and served from Newmarket in 1871. From 1872, an iron church was used and then, in 1877, the church of Our Lady Immaculate and St. Philip Neri was opened.

HAVERHILL was founded from Kirtling. Mass was said in the Bell Hotel in 1896. In 1911, it was visited by the Motor Mission. It became a regular Sunday Mass centre in 1936, in the house of Mr Miller. In 1938, the temporary chapel of St. Felix and St. Edmund was opened.

STOWMARKET. Fr Warmoll arrived there in 1879. There were six Catholics in the town. In 1884, the church of the Seven Dolours was opened with a school in its lower storey. A new presbytery was built in 1902 and the Ursuline nuns built a school, but it had to close later.

SUDBURY. In 1876, Canon Rogers at Coldham offered Mass at Sudbury. He made the long, fortnightly journey on horseback at first and then, later, in a 'buggy' with two horses in tandem. The first resident priest came there in 1880. A house and garden was purchased and a cottage was rented and converted into a chapel, containing 13 chairs. The Servants of the Sacred Heart started a home for the sick, poor, elderly or orphans. In 1893, the church of Our Lady and St. John the Evangelist was opened. At nearby ASSINGTON, the Brothers of the Christian Schools had their novitiate of St. Joseph's.

EAST BERGHOLT. The English Benedictine Nuns of Brussels moved from Winchester to East Bergholt in 1857 and set up a 'school for young ladies'. Their chaplains served as missioners in the district. When Bishop Wareing retired there in 1858, he caused a conventual church to be built with a side-chapel for externs. There was no sign of Catholic life in the district when the nuns arrived, but the retired Bishop Wareing went about making converts. Under government evacuation orders, the nuns left during the Second World War. The Franciscans bought the property and moved their house of studies there in 1946. The Friars had a Mass centre at FRAMLINGHAM.

STOKE and **NAYLAND.** There were three churches at STOKE and its Catholic history goes back to Penal times. The Mission there arose out of the Penal times' chapel at GIFFORD HALL, which, in 1843, had been the Diocesan Seminary before this was transferred to Northampton.

The writer, in the 'Centenary Souvenir', illustrates the attitude of Catholics in the Diocese in 1950 by his concluding words. ' *The number of places in which the Mass is occasionally said is legion. When we think of the small beginnings of many places ... we can hope that many future parishes are in their beginnings. But the day for that is far off. Meanwhile, priests say three Masses, make great efforts to say Mass in the Easter Duty period in distant villages and the Travelling Mission ... reaches the loneliest Catholics in the most isolated spots. The experience of the Travelling Missioner and of our priests in the country districts is that, although the going is still very hard, the propsects for the growth of the Faith in the future, and the not too distant future, are full of hope.*'

The Diocese of Northampton, 1851

The Diocese of Northampton, 1900

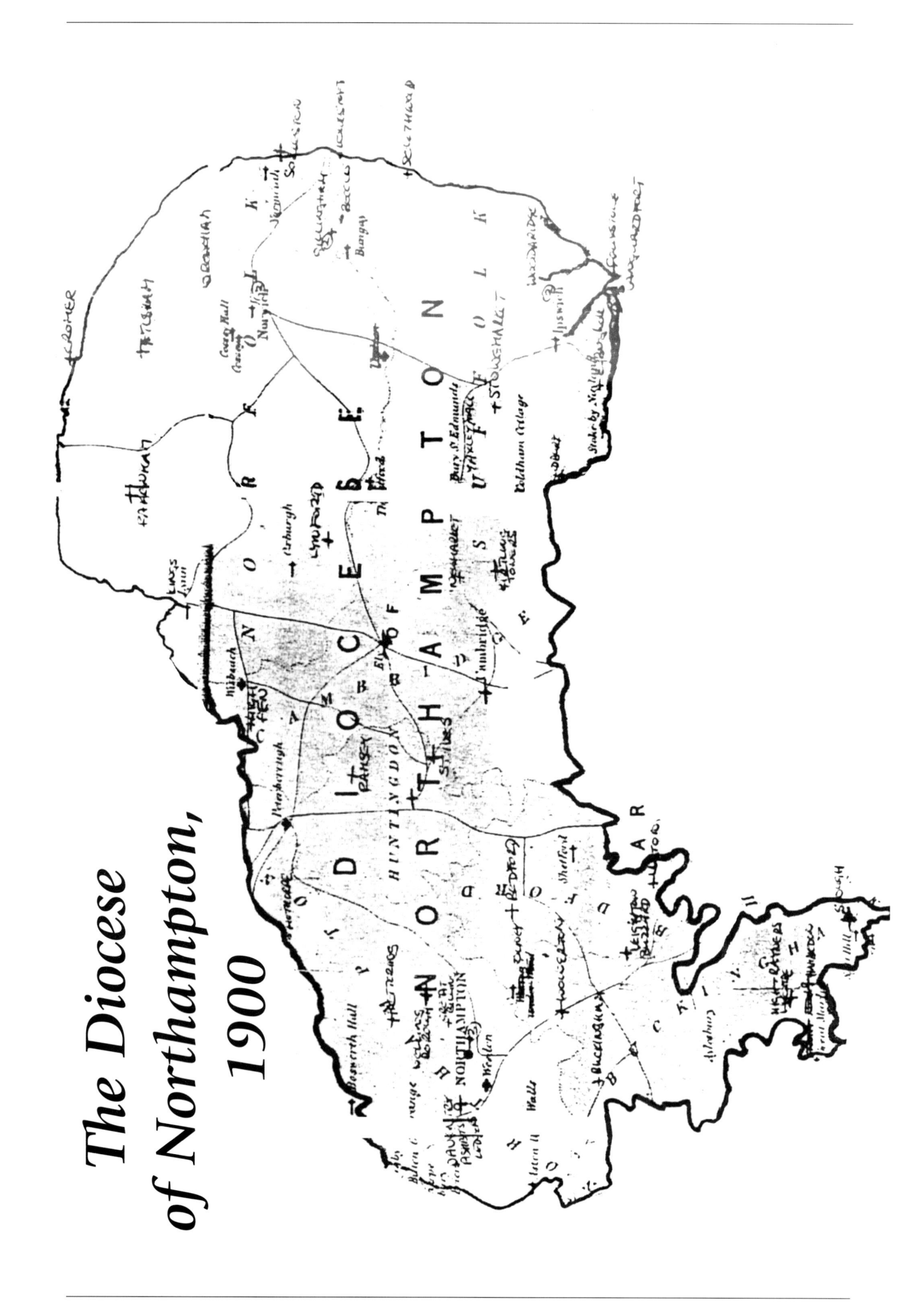

The Diocese of Northampton, 1950

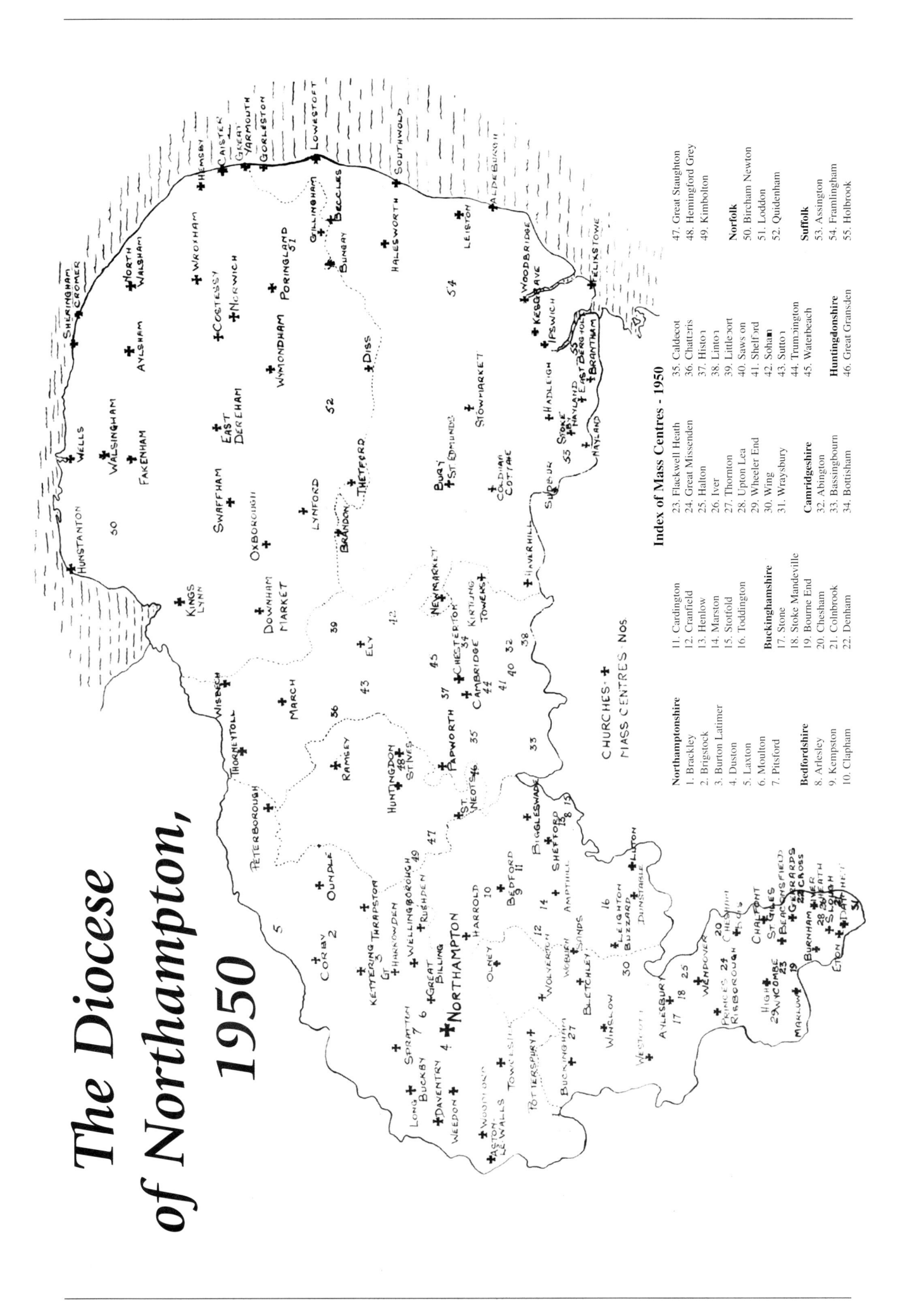

CHURCHES: ✚
MASS CENTRES Nos.

Northamptonshire
1. Brackley
2. Brigstock
3. Burton Latimer
4. Duston
5. Laxton
6. Moulton
7. Pitsford

Bedfordshire
8. Arlesey
9. Kempston
10. Clapham
11. Cardington
12. Cranfield
13. Henlow
14. Marston
15. Stotfold
16. Toddington

Buckinghamshire
17. Stone
18. Stoke Mandeville
19. Bourne End
20. Chesham
21. Colnbrook
22. Denham

Index of Mass Centres - 1950

23. Flackwell Heath
24. Great Missenden
25. Halton
26. Iver
27. Thornton
28. Upton Lea
29. Wheeler End
30. Wing
31. Wraysbury

Cambridgeshire
32. Abington
33. Bassingbourn
34. Bottisham
35. Caldecot
36. Chatteris
37. Histon
38. Linton
39. Littleport
40. Sawston
41. Shelford
42. Soham
43. Sutton
44. Trumpington
45. Waterbeach

Huntingdonshire
46. Great Gransden
47. Great Staughton
48. Hemingford Grey
49. Kimbolton

Norfolk
50. Bircham Newton
51. Loddon
52. Quidenham

Suffolk
53. Assington
54. Framlingham
55. Holbrook

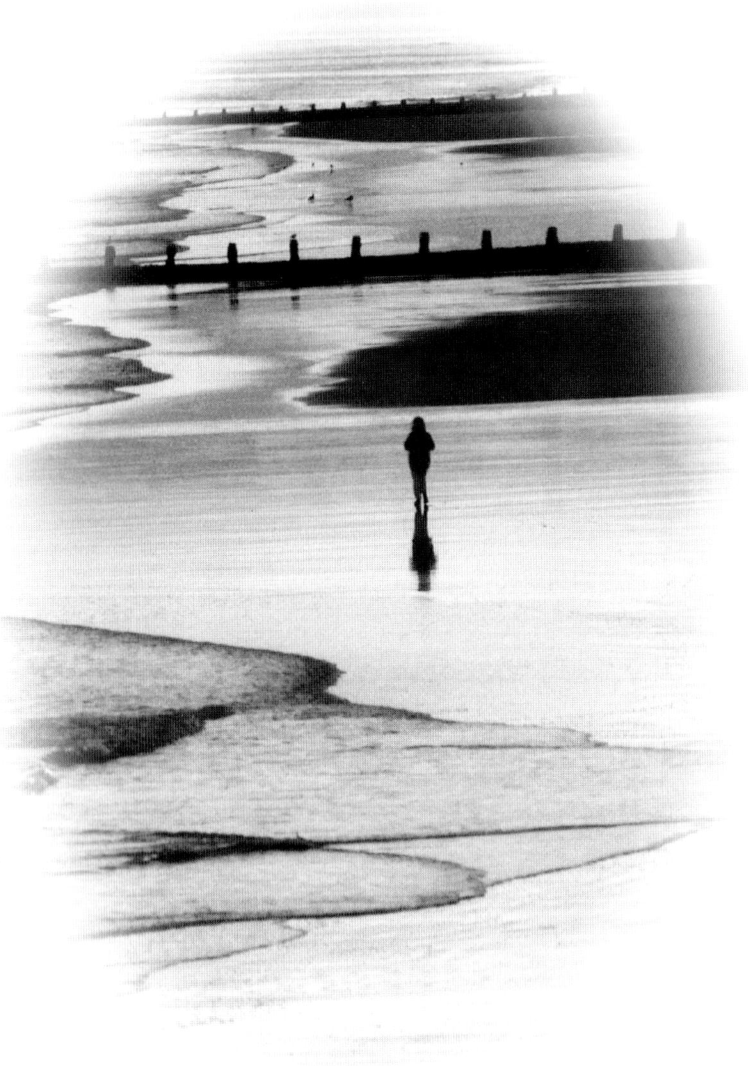

3.
Ten Bishops
- Personalities and Policies

Rt. Rev William Wareing (1850 - 1858)

Rt. Rev William Wareing

William Wareing was in his fifty-ninth year when he was made the first Bishop of Northampton in the restored English hierarchy of 1850.

Born in London on 16 February 1791, he had been ordained priest on 28 September 1815. Thus, his early years as a priest had been spent in a Catholic Church in England that was only slowly recovering from obscurity and near extinction. No doubt it was this early experience that made him missionary minded. Dedicated to building up the Church in the land, he worked to bring the people back to the Faith and to take the Mass to the scattered Catholics in the Eastern District.

After having taught at Oscott and Sedgley and having been a priest at Cresswell (Staffs), Grantham and Stamford, he had become the Vice-President of Oscott in1838. Two years later, in 1840, he was consecrated Bishop of Aristopolis, a nominal see, and moved to Northampton to be Vicar Apostolic of the Eastern District, which corresponded roughly to the future Northampton Diocese.

When, therefore, the Hierarchy was restored and William Wareing was made Bishop of Northampton, in a sense, not much had changed. He had been acting in that capacity, more or less, for the past ten years. And yet, in a more subtle way, things would now be different. Bishop Wareing now had, so to say, the title deeds. The Catholic Church in England was now more evident. No longer should the English Catholic body be seen as, in Newman's phrase, a *gens lucifuga*, a people who shunned the light of public notice.

It was Wareing's responsibility to bring the Church in this Diocese into the light and be an influence in society, while sensitively allaying the fears that had provoked the anti-Catholic outcry in 1850. He accomplished that task well.

It has been said that his vision was larger than life in some ways. He founded a Seminary and saw old St. Felix's as a 'Collegiate Church' with a body of ecclesiastics to sing the Divine Office and maintain a kind of spiritual citadel on Primrose Hill in Northampton in the spirit of the Cathedrals of mediaeval England. He also set up the Chapter of Canons and thus laid the foundations of the Northampton Diocese. The foundations were well laid. They made the subsequent development of the Diocese possible and strong.

Bishop Wareing retired in 1858 to East Bergholt with the community of Benedictine nuns. Even there he was driven by the missionary impulse and was to be seen stomping around the countryside making converts.

He died on 26 December 1865.

Rt. Rev Francis Kerril Amherst (1858 -1879)

Francis Amherst was a Bishop of different stock and different outlook from his predecessor. Born in London of an old aristocratic family from Essex on 21 March 1819, he has been described as, 'In the best possible sense a man of the world as well as a man of God and his horizon was as wide as the Catholic world.'

His first connection with Northampton was as a pupil in 1829 at Fr Foley's school next to the chapel of St. Felix - called rather grandly, an academy 'for the sons of gentlemen'. Amherst described the system of education there as, 'decidedly queer and eccentric'. At some point he joined the Third Order of St. Dominic. Such, then, were the influences that formed the future bishop.

He was ordained priest on 6 June 1846 and served for a time at Stafford. He was like Wareing in one respect in that he, too, taught at Oscott. And it was at St. Mary's Oscott that he was consecrated Bishop for Northampton on 4 July 1858.

The days of Catholics having to hide away and keep a low profile were over. They had enjoyed emancipation for three decades and had weathered the storm that had greeted the Restoration of the Hierarchy only eight years earlier. Now was the time for Bishops to be seen and to make their mark and Amherst was just the man to do that. This was evident in his manner of installation at Northampton. On 6 July 1858, he stopped at Weedon, one of the first missions in the area a few miles from Northampton. There the new Bishop was met by the Vicar Capitular and a member of the Northampton Chapter. He robed in the chapel and was conducted with great solemnity in a very handsome carriage to the Collegiate Chapel in Northampton where the rest of the Canons were present to greet him. A tent had been erected a short distance from the entrance to the church and, after the initial ceremonies, the Bishop and Canons proceeded to the church. The newspapers of the time reported that all were struck by the majestic ceremonial of his welcome and no less by his 'mild, holy and dignified appearance'. The Hierarchy was not only restored, it was now seen to be established. Symbols matter.

Rt. Rev Francis Kerril Amherst

It was doubtless the same instinct that inspired Bishop Amherst to undertake the great work of his episcopate, the partial rebuilding of the Cathedral and its inauguration as the Cathedral Church of Our Lady and St. Thomas. He had obtained a rescript from Rome, dated 15 September 1859, making the Immaculate Conception the co-titular of the Cathedral with St. Thomas of Canterbury.

But it was not all for show. Amherst not only continued to establish churches, but he also may be credited with founding the school system of the Diocese as well as setting up the orphanage at Shefford.

In 1879, Bishop Amherst resigned because of ill health and retired to Feildgate, Kenilworth with the title of Bishop of Sozusa. Four years later, on 21 August 1883, he died and was buried in his Northampton Cathedral.

Rt. Rev Arthur Grange Riddell (1880-1907)

Rt. Rev Arthur Grange Riddell

There is something strangely supernatural about the origins of Bishop Riddell. That he was born on 15 September 1836 in Paris into a Northumberland family was natural enough. But the supernatural element comes in when his mother, formerly the Honourable Catherine Stapleton of Charlton Towers in Yorkshire, took Arthur and her two other sons on a visit to the Curé d'Ars.

The saintly Curé told her that two of her sons would become priests and one would become a great dignitary in the Church. Widdington, her eldest son, became a Canon of the Middlesbrough Diocese and parish priest of Redcar, while her youngest son, Arthur, became Bishop of Northampton. In view of the prophecy, Mrs Riddell had purchased a pectoral cross, and a gold chain for it was bequeathed by his aunt, Miss Eliza Riddell, to whom Mrs Riddell had confided her secret, 'to be given to him on the day of his consecration'.

And so it was, when Arthur was consecrated Bishop of Northampton on 9 June 1880. Before that, he had been a priest (ordained 24 September 1858) at Hull and Scarborough. Aged forty-four and in vigorous health, Bishop Riddell threw himself into developing the Diocese and building on the foundations of his predecessors.

His stated policy was, *'to bring the Faith to the English people, to open missions and erect churches of moderate size, but of good design in new centres'*. *'For'*, he asked, *'is it not true that where our Divine Lord resides the light of faith is kindled or revives, sinners are drawn to repentance and the charity of devout people is largely increased?'*

Although his aims and motives were entirely spiritual, his means were very practical. Spectacularly grand churches could be built when outstandingly generous gifts were offered, such as St. John's Norwich paid for by the fifteenth Duke of Norfolk, or Our Lady and the English Martyrs at Cambridge, the gift of Mrs Lyne Stephens. But otherwise, apart from putting in something from his own means, Bishop Riddell's rule was that before anything should be done, two thirds of the money should be raised. He was not averse to stirring people's consciences and pockets, for example when in his Advent Pastoral of 1905 he pointed out that he has a magnificent plot in Luton purchased for £1,850 lying idle. In addition to this extraordinary church building programme, he established a Seminary and was very active for Catholic education.

He was also able to move out of the house, 'West View' in Semilong, which he could no longer rent, into the fine new Bishop's House in Marriott Street in 1885. This was the gift of that same benefactress Mrs Lyne Stephens, a French ballet dancer who had married the man who invented moveable doll's eyes and had made a fortune. The account for this house shows that the cost was £12,339 - 10s -9d, of which the Bishop had to contribute a mere £1 - 4s - 6d.

Towards the end of his time as Bishop, he could look back and see that he had largely fulfilled his aim of building up the Diocese. In 1905, it was noted that the Diocese had 70 priests, 35 parishes, 15 Mass stations and the Catholic population was estimated at 12,744. This means that by the end of his ministry, what are now the Dioceses of Northampton and East Anglia had gained nearly half of their present shape.

Bishop Riddell's episcopate could be characterised as one of brilliant administration, clear vision, steady growth. But this must not lead us to think of him as just a remote, cold administrator. In the Cathedral parish he was remembered as an indefatigable visitor of the people, a familiar figure accompanied by his large dog. He was most frequently referred to as simply, 'Good Bishop Riddell'. He died on his seventy-first birthday, 15 September 1907, and was buried in Northampton Cemetery and later reburied just outside the Cathedral. He had been Bishop for twenty-seven years.

Rt. Rev Frederick William Keating D.D. *(1908-1921)*

Bishop Keating was somewhat of a contrast to his predecessor. His background was Birmingham. Born there on 13 June 1859 and ordained priest on 20 October 1882, he taught at Olton, Marston Green Children's Home and Oscott.

After a year as Vice-Rector at Olton, he went as priest to Wednesbury in 1880 and ten years later was the Administrator at St. Chad's Cathedral, Birmingham. On 25 February 1908, he was consecrated Bishop of Northampton.

He in no way matched Bishop Riddell's record for building churches, although he did consecrate a number that Riddell had inaugurated. It is possible that the 1914 -18 War and its following period of reconstruction restricted church building during his episcopate. This, however, only accounts for the final years of his time. Church building was not really his thing nor, perhaps, the most pressing need of the time as he saw it.

It has been said that, 'He was a great churchman in the pattern of William Wykeham, striking in appearance and speech and in the broadness of his interests taking one back to the days of Bishop Amherst.' His forte, one might say, was the ministry of the word. His eloquent sermons drew crowds to Northampton Cathedral and his pastorals were sought after outside the Diocese. During the First World War he headed out to New York for the Episcopal Golden Jubilee of Cardinal Gibbons, the last survivor of the First Vatican Council, and he was sponsored by the British Government for a lecture tour of the United States.

An appreciation of his concern for Catholic culture may be gained from a Pastoral Letter of 1917 entitled, 'Catholic Culture and English Speech'. The situation is the war with hundreds of thousands of English speakers coming from 'The Empire' and the New World, many of them Catholic. He reflects on the prospect of the passing of 'The Empire', but the likely widespread endurance of the English language. He points out that 40,000,000 Catholics are English speaking worldwide, but that works like Dr Lingard's 'History' reach less than 1,000. He applauds Newman. But he points out, 'Our literature and the habits of thought it engenders and fosters are frankly non-Catholic, even when they are not openly anti-Catholic.

Rt. Rev Frederick William Keating D.D.

English theology is feeble and vacillating even when it happens to be orthodox. English philosophy is mostly sceptical and materialistic. English drama and fiction are mostly of the earth, earthy and English journalism may be relied upon to be anti-Papal.'

The Bishop reflects that the Latin language was once similarly pagan, but became the language of the Church. He looks for modern triumphs in English to equate those of Tertullian, St. Cyprian, St. Jerome and St. Augustine. Although at war with Prussia, he equates the 'Manchester School' as equally malign.

Perhaps, after all, Bishop Keating was not so different from Riddell. Cannot words as well as bricks be used to build up the Church? Finally, on 13 June 1921, Frederick Keating was translated to become the Metropolitan Archbishop of Liverpool and died on 7 February 1928 and was buried at Upholland.

Rt. Rev Dudley Charles Cary-Elwes (1921-1932)

Rt. Rev Dudley Charles Cary-Elwes

There is a homely feeling about Bishop Cary-Elwes. He was the first priest of the Diocese to be raised to the episcopate. Born at Nice on 5 February 1868, his family home was at Great Billing near Northampton.

Ordained on 30 May 1896, he served as a priest at Peterborough and Luton and as a Diocesan Schools Inspector. When he was consecrated Bishop of Northampton on 15 December 1921, the priests of the Diocese knew that here was a Bishop from among themselves who knew them, knew the Diocese and knew their hopes and problems.

Cary-Elwes had to rule a Diocese which was recovering from the war years in which changing habits of life were bringing new and great social and spiritual problems. The countryside was losing its remoteness through the motor-car and motor-bus. The country town was losing its prosperity through the centralising of industry and gaining a new type of parishioner through the dispersal of population in search of housing. He established a number of new missions and parishes.

He was a gifted musician, which skill brought him into a wider circle. He was charming and scrupulously accurate. He sends 'nearly £70' to the Pope for Peter's Pence and informs the Diocese in a Pastoral Letter, 'to be quite accurate £69 -18s - 10d' In that year, 1929, he rejoices that the Holy See has become 'The Vatican', a sovereign state after having lost the Papal States in the Risorgimento. He recalls that it is 100 years since Catholic Emancipation. He dwells at great length on the difficulties faced, on the heroism of clergy and laity and on the martyrdoms. Where would we be if put to a similar ordeal?

The Bishop urges the faithful to see in the Christ-Child the source of supernatural strength, the strength that has protected the successor of St. Peter. ' Though He was God ... He was to lead the martyrs along the way of death on to the tree of shame, changing thereby the ignominy into triumph, the gibbet into a pulpit whence the divine truth that out of true humility comes greatness of soul, out of seeming defeat comes glorious victory, might be preached to the whole wondering world.'

Bishop Cary-Elwes began the practice of the Annual Diocesan Pilgrimage to Lourdes. It was on one such pilgrimage that he took ill and died on 1 May 1932. He was buried in the churchyard at his family home of Great Billing.

Rt. Rev Laurence Youens (1933 - 1939)

Laurence Youens was another native of the Diocese. He was born in High Wycombe on 14 December 1873. But his first contact with the Diocese was when, as a boy curious about Catholicism, he cycled to a Catholic church to find Bishop Riddell addressing Confirmation candidates, after which he spoke with the Bishop.

He gave up the chance of going to Cambridge University and became a member of the Society of African Missionaries and was ordained priest on 30 June 1901 at Choubrah (Egypt) and then served as a missionary and taught at Zagazig (Egypt). It was there that a life-changing, terrible event occurred. He was nearly murdered.

Such was the traumatic effect of this that he suffered what today would be called a breakdown and so he returned to England and to his home town. From then on he worked in and for Northampton Diocese, first for five years as a curate in High Wycombe and then at the Shefford Catholic Boys' Home. During his years there he had cared for 1,650 boys and his earlier trials had wrought in him a marvellous sympathy for those boys. His care extended to helping them find work and he was greatly distressed when he learnt that some of them had been killed in the 1914-18 war.

On 25 July 1933, aged sixty, he was consecrated Bishop of Northampton, not something he had at all wanted. He lacked the physical distinction of some of his predecessors, but he had a greatness of heart, of humanity.

His terrifying ordeal in Egypt had left him with a fear of death, a vivid realisation of how terrible the concomitant circumstances might be. Now it was to be his destiny to be Bishop at the very time that war broke out in 1939. His fear of death translated itself into an immense compassion born of awareness of what people must face. He composed a Pastoral Letter urging people to practise their faith and say the Rosary at this difficult time. Mercifully, he was spared the full horror of that War, for he died on 14 November 1939.

What was there to show for his time as Bishop? Church building and the establishing of Mass centres had gone on apace although, perhaps, not so extensively as it had done under some of his earlier predecessors. Corby, Aylesbury, North Walsham, Ampthill and Gorleston are fitting monuments to him.

Rt. Rev Laurence Youens

Far more striking, however, than any material progress was the spiritual growth that he had encouraged in the Diocese. This is less easily reckoned, but a very clear mark was his restoration of the Slipper Chapel at Walsingham and the revival of Catholic devotion to Mary which, like the Slipper Chapel itself, had declined. His great moment was when, in 1934, he led about 10,000 Catholics from across the whole country to Walsingham for the first National Pilgrimage of Reparation. The vast gathering that moved in pilgrimage from the splendid church of St. John the Baptist in Norwich to Walsingham itself where, along with nine Bishops, Cardinal Bourne led them in prayer, could leave no one in doubt that there was a resurgence of faith. If Bishop Youens were to be remembered for this alone, that would be sufficient.

Rt. Rev Thomas Leo Parker M.A. *(1941 - 1967)*

Rt. Rev Thomas Leo Parker M.A.

After the death of Bishop Youens, the Diocese had to wait for more than a year for the appointment of his successor. This meant that the life of the Diocese slowed down and many things had to be put on hold.

All that changed, however, with the arrival on 11 February 1941 of Bishop Leo Parker. Now all was activity, growth, development. The Diocese reached its peak under his administration.

Leo Parker came with a wealth of experience and a clear vision of what was needed. Born in Sutton Coldfield on 21 December 1887, he had been ordained priest on 26 May 1916. After some years as secretary to the Bishop of Salford, he was priest at Higher Broughton. Always active in the cause of Catholic education, he had also been a member of the BBC Religious Affairs Committee. In 1940, he was honoured with the title of Domestic Prelate.

It was by no means an easy time in which to begin his episcopate. The war was at its height. There were frequent air raids in many parts of the Diocese, especially in East Anglia, and the splendid church of Our Lady and the English Martyrs in Cambridge, for example, received a direct hit from bombing. There was much evacuation and the presence of armed forces everywhere. Access to coastal areas was denied. Travel by train, so essential in this widespread Diocese, was restricted and most things, including petrol, were in short supply and rationed.

None of this, however, was going to stop Bishop Parker from exploring his Diocese and moving among his people to do God's work. It had its risks, of course. On one early occasion, he filled his car with maps and scrounged some petrol and set off to explore. Passing near a military airfield in some remote part of East Anglia, he was arrested on suspicion of being a spy and locked in a prison cell for the night. This may have offended his episcopal dignity of which he was very solicitous, but it did nothing to deter him from his task of caring for his Diocese.

During his twenty six years as Bishop, Leo Parker achieved a very great deal for the Diocese. The number of churches he opened was truly remarkable, especially when we remember that there were building restrictions for some time after the end of the War. His list of engagements is crammed with entries of visitations, confirmations and especially opening, blessing or consecrating churches. There is a record of his opening three new churches in one week and these were at widely scattered places.

Another theme that Bishop Leo constantly returns to in his Pastorals, sermons and exhortations is the need for Catholic schools and he was especially tireless in his battle to get a more just grant-aid from the government for Catholic schools. The increasingly favourable treatment given to Catholic voluntary aided schools is a mark of the considerable success of his efforts.

He had a great love for the Church and he felt strongly that the Catholic Church should be seen to be alive and prominent in this land. God should be worshipped in a place that was worthy. So it was that from early on in his episcopate, he set out to extend and glorify the Cathedral at Northampton. He spoke to the architect, Mr Albert Herbert, who had done such very good work at Mount St. Bernard's Abbey, and then he asked, cajoled and sought in any way possible to raise the necessary funds. He looked for support not only from the Catholics in the Diocese, but from anyone abroad who might help.

He gained a reputation for being a scrounger. There is a story of how once at lunch during the War the host, a farmer, promised the Bishop some grain for the chickens at Bishop's House. After lunch the Bishop, before getting into the car, said, 'We do not see our grain.' The farmer promised to send it on. 'We'll have it now' said the Bishop. 'A bird in the hand is worth two in the bush.' Or the story of the tramp who asked the Bishop for sixpence. After earnest discussion, the tramp put his hand in his pocket and gave the Bishop sixpence for the Priests' Training Fund.

It is said that convents expecting a visit from Bishop Leo would hide away pieces of furniture, carpets and other effects as they rightly feared he might say, 'We rather like that. It will look very well at Bishop's House or the Cathedral.'

The point is that Bishop Parker was not scrounging for personal gain, but for his beloved Diocese. His episcopal motto was 'Deus Providebit' (God will provide), but Bishop Parker knew that God needed a helping hand and that God's provision might not be delivered directly to Bishop's House doorstep.

His care for the Diocese engaged his attention on practical details. He was, for instance, an expert on drains, from some experience in Bishop's House, Salford, and would always enquire about the drainage system on visiting a new place. But he was even more assiduous in his concern and care for his clergy. He knew them well and was attentive to their needs. He was known not just for his building programme, or his monument of the Cathedral, or for the honour of being appointed in 1966 Assistant to the Pontifical Throne, but quite simply for his tremendous devotion to his vocation as Bishop.

After monumental labours, he retired first in Bishop's House and then at Fox Den, a pleasant place on the edge of Burnham Beeches. He died on 25 March 1975 and was buried in his Cathedral in the habit of the Franciscan Order to which he had been affiliated in gratitude for all he had done for the Franciscans.

Rt. Rev Charles Alexander Grant M.A., L.C.L. (1967-1982)

Rt. Rev Charles Alexander Grant M.A., L.C.L.

Charles Grant became Bishop of Northampton when the Church was experiencing a period of great change. It fell to him to manage that change as it affected the Diocese and to keep the Diocese together as it moved into the post-Vatican II world. Fortunately, his experience and personal qualities fitted him to achieve that with a considerable degree of success.

He and the Diocese knew each other very well. It was in Cambridge that he was born (25 October 1906), grew up and became a Catholic at the age of fourteen, graduated at the University and served for some time as a priest. There were two further appointments as priest at Ely and Kettering. Having done further studies in Canon Law in Rome, he worked for a time for the Diocesan Marriage Tribunal and raised its standard of efficiency. In 1955, he became Vicar General and in 1960 was honoured with the title of Domestic Prelate and then, in 1961, he was made Auxiliary Bishop to assist Bishop Leo Parker. In 1967, he succeeded Leo as Bishop of Northampton.

Thus it was that he accompanied Bishop Parker to the Second Vatican Council and there Bishop Grant made a speech on the subjects of the developing nations and peace, with particular emphasis on poverty and the immorality of nuclear weapons of mass destruction. He said that on its attitude to these questions the Council would be largely judged by the world. This speech contributed to the Council's 'Constitution on the Church in the Modern World'. This was followed by Pope Paul VI's encyclical 'Populorum Progressio' and his setting up the Pontifical Commission for Justice and Peace. Similar National Commissions were formed and Bishop Grant was appointed president of the Commission for England and Wales. He was instrumental in the development of CAFOD and CIIR.

Back in the Diocese, Bishop Grant continued to spread the message of the Council and Justice and Peace groups have flourished. But, of course, this was not the only aspect of the Church's life that Vatican II promoted. So Bishop Grant worked to put into effect the reforms in the Liturgy. This he did energetically but with sensitivity, and he had to deal with considerable opposition at times, especially in the widely publicised conflict over the new form of Mass centred on Fr Oswald Baker at Downham Market. It is to Bishop Grant's credit that he managed to settle that crisis without too many casualties.

It was in his nature to defuse crisis situations and to be respectful and sensitive to people of whatever rank or position. He had a reputation, when a parish priest, of being good to curates. Indeed, as Bishop it was in defending curates' rights that he had a row with his first Vicar General who went off in a huff. And many priests could give accounts of how Bishop Grant dealt kindly and justly with them when they were in various sorts of trouble. His most frequent exhortation to his priests was, 'be kind'.

He knew his Canon Law thoroughly, but he recognised that the law existed for the benefit of people, not to crush them. Although he was clear and firm on matters of principle, he paid special attention to the footnotes on pastoral considerations.

At one clergy Deanery meeting, a certain priest, quite irrelevantly to the matter in hand, suddenly appealed to Bishop Grant to join him in condemning some priests who had been observed in what he loudly asserted was a disgraceful act - ' they are not wearing the girdles round their albs! Surely they must be disciplined?' Charles, from the depth of his armchair, replied quietly, but authoritatively, ' The documents from Rome are quite clear. They prescribe freedom.' When, on another occasion, someone complained of girl altar servers at some churches, Bishop Grant said, *'You know, as I go around and see all those boy altar servers, I notice that they now all have long hair. And sometimes I see some even have ribbons in their hair.'* Charles held the law in high regard, but he had no time for petty legalism.

In the spirit of Vatican II, he avoided triumphalism. Unless the occasion demanded that he dress in official garb, you would be more likely to find him in very ordinary, casual attire. His lifestyle was frugal almost to a fault. While at seminary at Oscott, he had made a vow with some other seminarians never to complain about material circumstances in the ministry. As a priest and bishop, he refused to get a new car. At the time before the three-year M.O.T. test, a passenger in his car could see disconcertingly through holes in the floor the ground speeding by. While the outside of Bishop's House was to be kept weatherproof, the Bishop's rooms were not to be redecorated. Indeed, the carpet wore through to the floorboards where the Bishop sat.

He had a bad heart from the age of forty and his later years were marked by what he called 'a plethora of minor ailments' - cataracts, gallstones, bronchitis and various other afflictions including a mild stroke from which he recovered. He seemed to become increasingly tired as time went on and, although he had the assistance of his Auxiliary Bishop Alan Clark, he found it more and more difficult to carry out his work as he would have wished. But although he more frequently now declined invitations to various events, he would with great effort set off to a Confirmation or Ordination, for example, even though feeling rotten.

Charles Grant had brought the Diocese pretty well unscathed through the difficult, even turbulent period of Vatican II. He had set in motion a higher degree of financial and organisational centralisation by his gift of delegation. In his day computers had made their first appearance and he used Bishop's House to provide a centre not just for finances, but for the Marriage Tribunal and a Youth Office.

In 1976, the Diocese was divided with the Eastern half forming the new Diocese of East Anglia and with Alan Clark as its first Bishop. Charles Grant soldiered on in Northampton until he retired to Kiln Green (Reading) in 1982. He died on 24 April 1989 and was buried at Woburn Sands.

Rt. Rev Francis Gerard Thomas (1982 - 1988)

Rt. Rev Francis Gerard Thomas

The Diocese had great hopes when it was learnt that Bishop Grant's successor was to be Frank Thomas, as he was generally referred to. He was relatively young at fifty-two, respected as a theologian and it was fairly widely known that he was Bishop Grant's favoured candidate. Unfortunately, his programme of building on Bishop Grant's work and of developing the Diocese was cut short by his premature death.

Francis Thomas came from Stone in Staffordshire, where he was born on 29 May 1930 and he was ordained priest on 5 June 1955. After a short spell in the parish of Leamington Spa, he had made further studies in Rome and then, in 1959, taught at Oscott, Theology and particularly Liturgy. In 1968, he became Rector of Oscott where we got to know him well because of the Diocese having many of its ordinand students there. It was while he was parish priest at Newcastle-under-Lyme, where he had gone in 1979, that he was invited to become Bishop of Northampton. He was consecrated Bishop on 29 September 1982.

A former Bishop's Secretary writes, *'If Grant had been tired, Thomas, on arrival, was like a spring springing. Bishop Thomas arrived to the dust of Bishop's House and set in motion everything that could be moved. Interested in every detail, he was acutely conscientious. His desk became piled high with tasks taken on personally. He drove to Downside one morning and Bedford in the evening'.* The Church in Milton Keynes was still growing and Bishop Thomas was closely involved with the ecumenical developments there.

He set in motion a Diocesan Pastoral Congress, called the Diocesan Assembly. It started off as an idea for the clergy, but ended up engaging the laity fully. There were two years of preparation with study weeks for the clergy and several meetings, both local and diocesan-wide, for the laity representatives. The climax was to be a weekend Assembly in May 1988. But, to the dismay of all, Bishop Thomas fell ill in the February and was operated on for cancer. He seemed to be recovering and gathered what strength he could to attend the Assembly weekend. The Assembly was a success in its time and many plans and resolutions were formed, although some people may have had expectations that were too high, or unrealistic.

Shortly after, however, Bishop Thomas had a recurrence of cancer and returned to the Bon Secours hospital in Beaconsfield. He continued to be our Bishop, but had to learn to delegate and decide. In sickness, he shared his thoughts by letter to the consolation and encouragement of many. He died on 25 December 1988, aged only 58, and was buried at Great Billing. His loss was deeply felt, not least by Bishop Grant, still then living in retirement.

Rt. Rev Patrick Leo McCartie (1990-)

To the sense of loss experienced by the Diocese on the death of Bishop Thomas was added a feeling of frustration and, indeed, abandonment. It was well over a year before the appointment of Bishop Leo McCartie to Northampton was announced. As one young girl wrote in a letter of welcome, 'What kept you?' No one seemed to know the answer to that, except that it was not Bishop Leo's fault.

Throughout the long period of waiting the Diocese, and especially the clergy, had become, perhaps, a bit dispirited. So Bishop Leo was faced with the task of putting new heart into the clergy and people. Looking back over the ten years or so of his episcopate, we can see that he did just that. Whatever else, this surely must be reckoned as his most telling achievement.

Leo McCartie came with long experience of being a priest and also a Bishop. He was born in 1925 in West Hartlepool, Co. Durham, but all his priestly life had been spent in the Archdiocese of Birmingham. After studying at Oscott, he was ordained priest on 17 July 1949 at St. Teresa's Church, Trent Vale, Staffordshire. One year as assistant priest was followed by six years (1950 - 56) on the teaching staff at Cotton College and as assistant priest in St. Wilfrid's, Cotton. After relatively brief spells as assistant priest at St. Chad's Cathedral, Birmingham, Wolverhampton and then Wednesbury, he was Diocesan Inspector of Schools from 1962 to 1968. This, of course, was the time of Vatican II and the new developments in Catechetics which Fr Leo helped to promote. He was Administrator of St. Chad's Cathedral, Birmingham when, on 20 May 1977, he was ordained Titular Bishop of Elmham as Auxiliary Bishop of Birmingham to Archbishop Dwyer. And then, on 19 March 1990, he was installed as the tenth Bishop of Northampton.

Bishop Leo's friendly and optimistic nature immediately commended him to the Diocese. The fact that he listened to clergy and people and energetically set about getting to know the Diocese, rather than coming with preconceived ideas, inspired confidence.

He signalled that one of his high priorities was to build up the clergy when, in the evening of the very day of his own installation as Bishop, he travelled to Aylesbury to ordain a priest. He has continued to foster priestly vocations and to care for the welfare of his present priests. Northampton Diocese had already taken something of a lead in ordaining both single and married men to the permanent Diaconate and this was a development that Bishop Leo encouraged. After the Synod of the Church of England had voted to allow the ordination to the priesthood of women, a number of Anglican priests, many of whom were married, sought to be ordained in the Catholic Church. Bishop Leo was very much involved with this matter. Not only did he receive into the Diocese and ordain several ex-Anglican priests, but he was also appointed by the Episcopal Conference to the National Panel of three Bishops who had the task of scrutinising and judging the applications for ordination of all ex-Anglican married priests in England and Wales. He carried this out in such a sensitive way that not only were these new priests in his Diocese warmly accepted by the clergy and people, but also his very good ecumenical relations with the Anglicans were in no way harmed.

Rt. Rev Patrick Leo McCartie

Those ecumenical relations with other churches had already been established by Bishop Leo's predecessors, Grant and Thomas. This was particularly the case in the new town of Milton Keynes where there were shared churches and ecumenical projects. Bishop Leo built on that and a high point was when the Queen and Cardinal Hume took part in a joint ecumenical occasion in Milton Keynes.

Since Vatican II, the Catholic Church has been looking beyond its own boundaries. This increased involvement in ecumenical co-operation was one sign of this, but it didn't stop there. Following the lead given by the Second Vatican Council's 'Constitution on the Church in the Modern World', the Church was sharing the concerns of society at large and contributing to the dialogue on social, economic and political matters.

Whereas formerly, for example, the Church had focused on the fight for the provision and funding for Catholic schools now, in addition to maintaining a high quality of Catholic education, it was concerned with education in general in the wider community and at all levels. Bishop Leo was alert to this and encouraged the Diocese and especially the laity to get involved. One sign of the acknowledgement of his contribution in this sphere was his being awarded the Honorary Degree of Doctor of Laws from Leicester University in recognition of the support he had given to the developing Nene College in Northampton, which was affiliated to Leicester University.

This mission of the Church in secular society belongs, of course, primarily to the laity. Bishop Leo carried forward some of the conclusions of the Diocesan Assembly to strengthen the role of the laity in the Diocese. For example, we saw the setting up of Diocesan, Deanery and Parish Pastoral Councils.

Unlike several of his predecessors, Bishop Leo did not open many new churches. In fact, some were closed and parishes began to be clustered because of shifting populations and a slight decline in the number of priests. However, there were several churches that were reordered to make them more fitted to the revised liturgy.

Probably the most notable of these was the Cathedral. In 1999, the Cathedral was extensively reordered, especially the Sanctuary and the Blessed Sacrament Chapel. It was in this splendid setting that Bishop Leo celebrated the Golden Jubilee of his Priesthood.

Bishop Leo is still happily with us, but is due to retire in the year 2000. Our prayer then will be, firstly for his continued happiness and well being, secondly that the Diocese will be given a successor who is at least as good as these ten very good Bishops we have had, and thirdly that we will not be kept waiting too long for that next Bishop to be appointed.

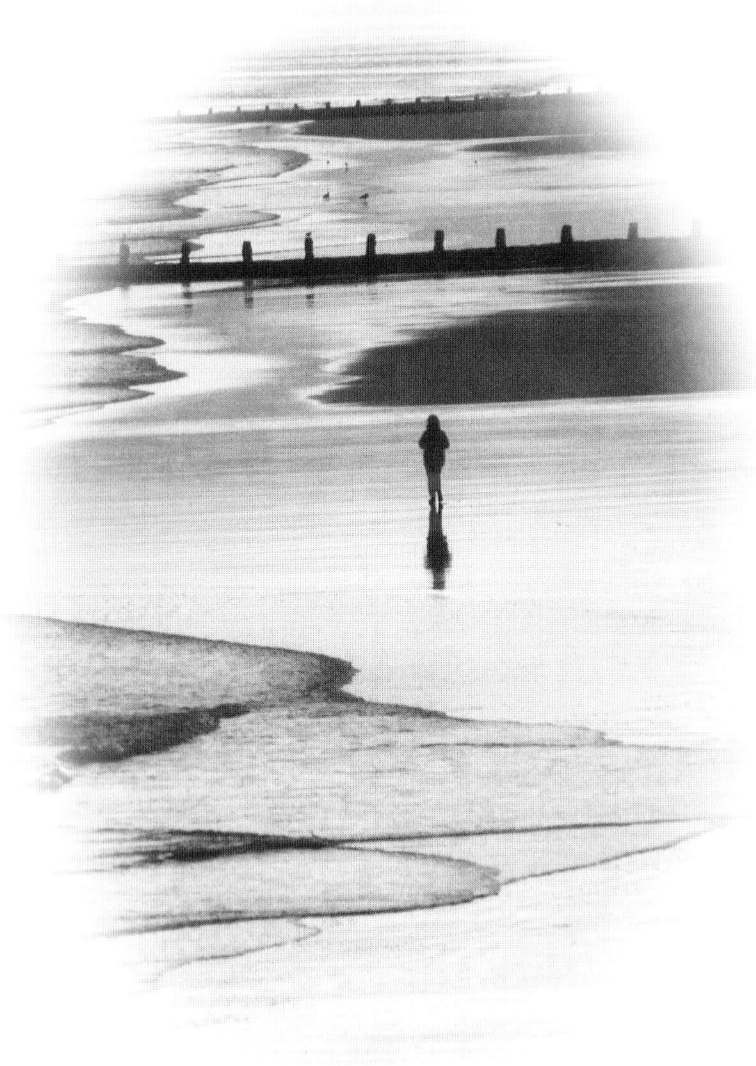

4.
The Council Years (1950-1975)
❖

When the Diocese celebrated its centenary in 1950, the war had been over for five years, but its effects were still being felt.

Domestic Chapel at Sawston Hall, with USA forces in occupation during the War

Reconstruction

Many people had been hoping that, with the end of hostilities, life would return to normal, by which they meant how it was before the War. This, however, was not to be. It could not be. The changes in society, that the War had effected, were too profound to be reversed. Of course, hundreds of civilians had been killed in air raids and large areas of cities had been destroyed, but that was not all. Society itself had been shaken out of its former mould. People of different classes, varying beliefs and from diverse communities had been thrown together in the Forces, in war work, as evacuees, or just by sharing the common peril. Attitudes and beliefs, even prejudices, had been questioned and challenged. Things could never be the same. Perhaps then, it was hoped, they could be better.

The programme now was not restoration, but 'post-war reconstruction'. This meant reconstructing not just houses, buildings, cities, but society itself. The 1944 Education Act aimed to restructure and revitalise education, and the National Health Service was the proud boast of the newly emerging Welfare State. The symbol and embodiment of this hoped-for future was the Festival of Britain in 1951.

To achieve this reconstruction would not be easy. World War II might have ended, but real peace had not yet been secured. The Cold War, with its Iron Curtain, now dominated and divided Europe. Many Allied and British Armed Forces, which included many young National Servicemen, were still stationed in Europe, trying to establish peace, while others were embarking to fight in the Korean war. And always, near at hand, was the fear and threat of nuclear conflict. Back home, the resources needed for any reconstruction were limited. Some things were still rationed, others were in short supply and building was subject to tight regulation.

This was the context in which the Catholic Church in Britain, and therefore the Diocese, had to live and carry out its mission and ministry. But it was not just the context that was changed. The Church was not separate and insulated from the contemporary society. Catholics had gone through the same experiences and were now affected by the same influences and constraints as were others. Moreover, those experiences and influences began to affect the way in which the Church now saw itself, its relationship with other Christians and with the increasingly secularised society. This, in turn, would lead the Church into new ways of thinking, of worship and of action. Although it was not evident at that time, the journey towards the Second Vatican Council had begun.

For the moment, however, the Church was in a mood to celebrate. 1950 was proclaimed a Holy Year and the dogma of Mary's Assumption into Heaven was solemnly defined by Pope Pius XII.

Preparing for the Holy Year

To prepare for this Holy Year - The Great Year of Jubilee - the Hierarchy, in a joint Pastoral Letter, ordered a general parochial Mission in all the parishes of the country in 1949. The organisation of this was entrusted to the Catholic Missionary Society, headed by Fr John Heenan (the future Cardinal Archbishop of Westminster). The priests of the Catholic Missionary Society would tour the country with their Trailer Chapel and bring the Mass and Sacraments to towns and villages. Their preaching and talks attracted crowds to the services and meetings. Missions were arranged for places throughout the Diocese, such as Northampton, Aldburgh, Cambridge, Daventry, Hollesley Bay, Luton, March, Newmarket, Norwich, Oundle, Southwold, Thrapston, Wellingborough, Yarmouth and many more.

Although the Catholic Missionary Society organised the National Mission, their priests were too few to carry out the nationwide mission on their own. So, local clergy led the mission in many places and a great many priests, some from abroad and many giving up their holidays, helped for several weeks. In the lists of missions in the Northampton Diocese, there are some names of priests that have since become well known - Fr Clifford Howell S.J., Fr Wingfield Digby S.J., Fr John Heenan, Fr Godfrey Anstruther O.P., Fr Thomas Holland (later to be Bishop of Salford) and, from the Diocese, Fr J. H. Thomson (parish priest of Woodbridge) and Fr John Mossey (of Southwold).

The liaison officer in the Diocese, to co-ordinate the mission and relate to the Catholic Missionary Society, was Fr Anthony Hulme. By the time of the National Mission, he already held a unique position as the Diocesan Travelling Missioner and had been working as such for the past year.

Up until the early 1970s, the Diocese of Northampton operated a Travelling Mission to serve remote parts

The Travelling Mission

The Diocesan Travelling Mission was an initiative of Bishop Leo Parker. He floated the idea in an article in the Diocesan Year Book in 1946. Two years later, it became a reality and Fr Anthony Hulme began his work, travelling constantly by car or van, from his base at Ely, to the widely scattered villages and isolated homesteads throughout this vast Diocese.

4 - The Council Years (1950-1975)

When it began in July 1948, the Travelling Mission was launched as an experiment. It was the first of its kind in the country, with no model to follow. Sometime afterwards, a priest from Menevia Diocese came to observe and learn from the Northampton experience and then returned home to set up a similar Mission in his Welsh diocese. After six months, it was clear that the experiment was working and the Travelling Mission continued and developed for very many years. It holds a significant place in the history of the Northampton Diocese.

By van to remote villages

The reports that Fr Hulme gave of the Travelling Mission are full of interesting details that not only chronicle the work of the Mission, but also provide an insight into the life of Catholics in those counties at that time.

In 1948, he visited thirty-seven Catholics at Pigotts - 'full of memories of Eric Gill'. Several asked for arrangements to be made to begin instructions in the Faith, others to have their marriages consolidated and a number to have their children christened. The Missioner always needed somewhere to sleep and at Welford, the Church of England vicar put him up for the night. At Clare, Mass was said for eighteen people in an old monastic building, with its glorious old Catholic church, while at Trumpington, Mass was celebrated for fifty-one people, 'near the spot where Our Blessed Lady gave the scapular to Simon Stock'. At Lode, there were thirteen in the congregation for Mass that was celebrated in the 'Gun and Hare' public house.

Fr Hulme finished a month in Rome with a broadcast from the Vatican on the work of the Travelling Mission and was back to Norfolk for Christmas Day Mass at Ixworth for twelve people, Ampton for three and Diss for thirty-four. He had breakfast in Norfolk, lunch in Cambridge and tea in Northamptonshire, covering almost 150 miles in the day, mostly due to saying Mass next day in Northants at Walgrave for seven and Irthlingborough for sixty Catholics.

During the next year, after visiting many places, he was at Brigstock for thirty-four Catholics, with the Lithuanians praying in a small group before returning to Lyveden, 'which Lord Tresham built in the shape of a cross and adorned with symbols of the Passion, all in honour of the Sacred Heart'. There were fifty-two refugees from Eastern Europe at Weldon camp and eighteen at Rockingham, where the Missioner went around the huts ringing the server's bell to call the faithful to Mass. Conington, with fifty-four Catholics, was a small, Polish settlement and at Yaxley there were eighty-four in a hostel for workers in the London Brick Company kilns.

Mass was said in one house where a Catholic young woman was giving a home to her father who once led a mob who drove Fr (later Cardinal) Vaughan out of one of our towns. The arrival of the Missioner to offer Mass at Wickham Brook, saved one man a ten mile walk. Each Sunday he used to walk ten miles, fasting, to Mass and Holy Communion. On another occasion, a friendly vicar lent the Missioner hassocks with the melancholy remark that he didn't suppose a Roman priest would want to borrow anything from him.

Fr Hulme showed considerable ingenuity in seeking out Catholics. There was the Belisha Beacon lying in the road at Burton Latimer. Thinking it best to get an alibi when he collected the beacon, Fr Hulme asked two small boys what their names were. Both owned up to being Catholics. When he turned the beacon into the police station, he asked the police if, in return, they would do something for him. He was told that he had come to the right place and he got the names of several newcomers.

At Quy, a little girl asked the Missioner if he was the doctor. Fr Hulme replied, 'No. The doctor makes you better. I make you good.' This led to the girl's mother coming out to talk to Fr Hulme and putting him onto a local Catholic or two. He reported that one family had read in 'The Universe' of his forthcoming visit to a certain place. So they cycled eleven miles to be at Mass. He also said that there are always plenty of Catholics where there is new life, be it on a new estate, or amid squatters, or on a converted camp site.

Fr Hulme received a lot of help from non-Catholics. One, for instance, lent a bed so that he might have somewhere to sleep. He also received into the Church a convert, 'the turning point of whose spiritual odyssey was offering to bring Catholics to Mass when the Travelling Missioner was at his wit's end for transport'. There was the incident of the dog that was fond of children, having been brought up with evacuees. The children of the village took it round with them everywhere. One mother came to the owner and said she was sorry they had been taking it to a non-Catholic Sunday School . ' I thought, you being a Catholic ... .'

The Missioner's van - can become an altar

In 1952, Fr Hulme reported that 'Mass is said annually, or in a few cases oftener, at some 125 centres'. In the same report, he speaks of the Travelling Missioner's van, 'boldly labelled, capable of becoming an altar in those rare cases of need when the room, which is almost invariably forthcoming, is not available. It is also used very much for fetching people to Mass. On one occasion a double journey with it brought eighteen to a single Mass. Then the Travelling Mission got a mobile Trailer Chapel, a gift from a Liverpool merchant, Mr Wilson, who formerly lived in the Northampton Diocese. He and his partner, Mr Mather, were having six trailers built and the first was given to Northampton. It had 'seating for twenty-eight, ecclesiastical windows, permanent altar, tabernacle and throne and electric light. Its bell enables the Angelus to ring out again in this remote corner of England. The mobile church is stabled by a good friend of the Travelling Missioner, by the moat of Gifford Hall.'

The apostolate went beyond providing Mass. There was a great need for religious instruction for children, which was chiefly met by the work of the Catechists by post. Bendiction, for some a rare treat, was provided. There were Information Classes for non-Catholics, lantern lectures on Catholic subjects and special demonstrations for the children. At Finedon, there were the open-air Stations of the Cross. The local parish priest announced the time and place and got the Cell members to visit local Catholics and put up notices. Each Station in turn was projected onto a large screen, while the Travelling Missioner, armed with a loudspeaker and standing by the old stone that was the remains of the ancient Cross, led the meditations and prayers. Despite the rain, some sixty people stayed throughout, while another score put in an appearance for part of the time.

In 1953, Fr Hulme reported that very many centres had been visited and also that the Travelling Mission had had a stand at the Vocations Exhibition at Olympia. In that year, the Travelling Mission made its first visit to Sandringham to celebrate Mass out of doors at the van. One hundred and twenty Scouts of all nationalities attended, beside a score of local Catholics. One mother walked three miles carrying her six-month-old baby in her arms.

The National Mission of 1949, was, of course, exceptional, preparing for the Holy Year. On one occasion during this Mission, the number of obvious listeners to Fr Hulme's talk was few. But, after giving his talk, he took a stroll and counted eighty-seven open windows within earshot. No one came out of the nearby inn, but that someone had listened was proved by the fact that someone inside took a collection, 'better than some of our smaller parish collections', and sent it out.

The Summer Campaign took place more regularly and had great effect. During one Summer Campaign, a priest called on a parishioner whom all had agreed was hopeless. She proved the best attender at the evening Services, Mass and Sacraments. Towards the end of the week, her husband told the Missioner that she had been saying, 'I wish I was back where I was fifty years ago'. He said, 'Where was that?' She replied, 'I was being confirmed fifty years ago today.' At that moment the priest knocked at the door and all resistance to Grace collapsed. In the Summer Campaign in Northampton, Mass was said in a variety of places - small chapels, the Women's Institute at Brackley, the Post Office at Abthorpe - and services and talks were held on village greens. Finally, there was a great meeting in the Market Square in Northampton. In 1950, it was reported that, during the Summer Campaign, 30 to 40 small towns and villages had had a resident priest in them for periods of up to a fortnight. In some there was a chapel, or Mass centre and in some, not even that. Mass was sometimes said in isolated homes. Attendance at Mass, talks in the evening and visits to the Blessed Sacrament, numbered over 20,000. More than 2,000 homes had been visited during the year in some 600 villages. Mass had been celebrated in some 70 centres, mostly new ones. Several had been visited more than once and most would remain open to an annual visit only. Some of the more successful ones, such as Framlingham, Diss and Loddon, were then being manned by local clergy as monthly, or even weekly, Mass centres. Fr Hulme concluded that, 'no village now but has its Catholic'.

The Travelling Mission continued for many years and Fr Hulme was given an assistant, Fr Manley, and eventually was replaced by Fr McCormack. In 1961, Fr McCormack was reconstructing a new chapel - a second-hand, single deck, diesel bus, converted into a Mobile Chapel. It would have a permanent altar, Stations of the Cross, church-type seating, allowing kneeling as well as seating space for 34 adults and window pictures to give the impression of stained glass windows. Appeals in 'The Universe' for money to pay for the refurbishment of the bus resulted in, among others, a donation from Zanzibar, East Africa.

Church Building

The Travelling Mission could not be, and was not intended to be, a permanent, or even long term, solution to the problem of making Mass available to the Catholics in the growing Diocese. What was needed were more settled parishes and proper churches. Bishop Parker set to, with his characteristic determination, to build and open new churches, to replace temporary churches with new permanent ones, to consecrate others and to raise what had been missions to the status of canonically established parishes. Towards the end of his time as Bishop, Leo Parker once said that he could not recall just how many churches he had built or opened. There were so many.

Bishop Leo Parker

The following list may not be complete, but it does give a clear indication of the scale and geographical spread of his achievement.

1950 -	WALSINGHAM. Temporary chapel of the Annunciation opened.
	GREAT YARMOUTH. St. Mary's consecrated.
	HALESWORTH. New chapel of St. Augustine blessed.
	NORWICH. St. Boniface temporary church opened and blessed.
	LUTON. Sacred Heart church opened and blessed.
	WESTCOTT. Church blessed.

1951 -	WENDOVER. Church at London Road opened.
	EAST DEREHAM. New church blessed.

1952 -	OLNEY. Church consecrated.
	DISS. Holy Trinity church blessed.

East Dereham

1953 -	BEDFORD. Christ the King church hall for Mass.
	LEIGHTON BUZZARD. New church opened.
	CHESHAM BOIS. Church extension blessed.
	NORTHAMPTON. St. Patrick's church opened.
	NEWPORT PAGNELL. Chapel of St. Bede opened.
	NORWICH. Holy Apostles church hall for Mass.

1954 -	WELLINGBOROUGH. Church of Our Lady consecrated.
	NORTHAMPTON. St. Gregory's church blessed.

1955 -	NORTHAMPTON. St. John's church rearranged and extended.

1956 -	WOBURN SANDS. New church opened and blessed.
	WRAYSBURY. Church.
	BLETCHLEY. New church of St. Thomas Aquinas opened.
	KETTERING. Church of St. Luke blessed.
	CORBY. St. Brendan's (hut and school).
	BOURNE END. Wooden church opened.
	LUTON. St. Margaret's hall completed for Mass.
	QUIDENHAM. New church blessed.

1957 -	HIGH WYCOMBE. New church of St. Augustine opened.
	BRACKLEY. Church.
	SLOUGH. Holy Family became a separate parish.
	YELVERTOFT. Church.
	NORWICH. St. John's consecrated.

Brackley

1958 -	BURNHAM. Church opened.
	BEDFORD. Clapham Park convent chapel blessed.
	IVER. Church blessed.
	LUTON. St. Margaret's became a parish.
	STONY STRATFORD. Church of St. Mary Magdalene.

1959 -	NORTHAMPTON. Cathedral enlarged.

Bridgettine Convent, Iver

4 - The Council Years (1950-1975)

| | LUTON. Church of Our Lady enlarged.
| | ROTHWELL. Church.

1960 - BEDFORD. Church of Christ the King blessed.
       CHESHAM. Church.

1961 - HARROLD. New church opened.
       NORTHAMPTON. Church of St. Margaret opened.
       BEDFORD. St. Joseph's new church.

1962 - BURNHAM. Church consecrated.
       CORBY. St. Brendan's church opened and blessed.
       HALTON. Church.
       LUTON. St. Martin de Porres mission started.
       ROADE. Church blessed.

1963 - BIGGLESWADE. New presbytery.
       GERRARDS CROSS. Church completed and opened.
       HOUGHTON REGIS. Church hall blessed.
       LONG CRENDON. Mission started. Resident priest.

1964 - SLOUGH. New church of St. Anthony opened.
       THRAPSTON. New church blessed.
       GREAT MISSENDEN. Church opened.
       CADDINGTON. Church.
       NORTHAMPTON. St. Aidan's church opened.
       AYLESBURY. Guardian Angels church blessed.
       DUNSTABLE. New church opened.
       ETON WICK. Church blessed.
       MARSTON. Church.

1965 - BEDFORD. St. Frances Cabrini church opened.
       HADDENHAM. New church in converted building.
       LITTLE CHALFONT. Church.
       LUTON. Holy Ghost church blessed.
       BLETCHLEY. New church of All Saints.

1966 - AYELSBURY. St. Clare church hall.
       LUTON. Church of St. John blessed.

The Bishop laying the foundation stone of the new church of St. Anthony, Farnham Royal, Slough, 1960

St. Mary's, Dunstable

Charles Grant became Bishop in 1967, when Bishop Parker retired, but the programme of building and development in this period up to 1975 continued.

1967 - BEDFORD. Church of Ss. Philip and James opened.
       RAUNDS. Church opened.

1968 - CAMBRIDGE. Church of St. Laurence.
       THRAPSTON. Became joint parish with Raunds.
       EARLS BARTON. Church blessed.

SLOUGH. Holy Family church consecrated.

1969 - SLOUGH. Church of the Holy Redeemer blessed.
NORWICH. New altar at convent consecrated.

1970 - BEDFORD. Ss. Philip and James became a separate parish.
HIGH WYCOMBE. New church of St. Wulstan.
LAXTON HALL. Polish Franciscans arrive.
MARLOW. Extended church opened and blessed.

1971 - WEEDON. New church, new site.
LONG BUCKBY. New church opened.
LONG CRENDON. New church opened.
OUNDLE. New church of The Holy Name. New site.

1972 - BURTON LATIMER. Church blessed.
DOWNLEY. Church of Our Lady and St. Augustine blessed.
DESBOROUGH. Church.
WELLINGBOROUGH. Church of Edmund Campion opened.

1973 - BIGGLESWADE. New church.

1974 - BUCKINGHAM. New church blessed.
MILTON KEYENES. St. Augustine. Mass begun in parish.

1975 - HIGH WYCOMBE. Downley shared church opened.
MILTON KEYNES. St. Augustine's. Mass in Christian Church Ecumenical Centre.

Further Expansion

The need for more new churches and, indeed, for schools and all else that goes with a parish, was made more acute by the growth of towns in the Diocese. There had been more industry in places like Luton, Northampton, Slough and others and there was a projected increase in the population of the new expansion areas in the Diocese.

In February 1971, Bishop Grant called all the clergy to a meeting to face the problems this posed and especially to find ways of meeting the cost. It was estimated that the Catholic population of the Diocese would increase in the next ten years by 40,000 new people coming into the four expansion areas of Milton Keynes, Northampton, Wellingborough and Peterborough. Ten new parishes would be needed. The rate of growth would be so rapid that the newly arrived could not possibly be expected to provide their own churches. Nor would finance from the newcomers and from Catholics already living in the expansion areas be sufficient to meet the cost.

Therefore, the Diocese must help. As Bishop Grant said, 'I am responsible for these people, and you, the presbyterium, and the whole Diocese share the responsibility. There is no one else to whom they can turn for help.' But the Diocese did not have anything like the income needed for this and so new sources of income had to be found. It was estimated that an income of £40,000 a year over the next ten years would enable the Diocese to provide half the cost of new churches and prebyteries. The other half and the whole cost of schools would have to be met by the newcomers and the people already living in the development

Bishop Grant

Church of St. Edmund Campion, Wellingborough

areas. Bishop Grant proposed to ask each parish for 50p each year for each Catholic attending Mass. He also said that the amount raised in the Advent collection for new and poor missions would count towards the quota and he thought the clergy could increase the collection, 'especially if we contribute ourselves. I propose to give £50 a year.'

The first new building in the Diocese to receive the 50% Diocesan grant, was the new church at Wellingborough. It was planned to accommodate 200 people. Since, however, the church was built as part of a new Catholic Infant school, it could be opened up on to the school hall, thus doubling the capacity of the church.

These were the hard realities of the spiritual growth of the Diocese.

Schools

Education has always been a priority of the Catholic Church. Certainly, from its beginning, the Northampton Diocese has had a great care for its schools and the Catholic people have made immense sacrifices to establish and support them.

Our second Bishop, Francis Amherst, went round the better off of the Diocese and managed to raise £50,000 for a start. Possibly no one was more determined that the Catholics should have their schools than Bishop Leo Parker and he fought unrelentingly to get a more just arrangement for State Grant Aid for Catholic schools.

The case for Catholic schools was based on law. This was clearly stated in the Diocesan Directory of, for example, 1956. It declared, 'Catholic parents have a solemn obligation before Almighty God to have their children taught their religion. There must be Catholic teachers in Catholic schools for Catholic children, whenever a sufficient number can be assembled to make this possible. That is the law of God and it is the law of the Church.' And Canon 1347 of the Code of Canon Law was quoted - 'Catholic children are not to attend non-Catholic schools, nor are they to go to schools of mixed religion, that is to such schools as are open also to non-Catholic children. It is for the Bishop, acting on instructions from the Holy See, to decide in what circumstances and under what safeguards against the danger of perversion to the pupils, attendance at such schools can be tolerated.' It was further stated that English Law recognised this right. But, and here was the fact that so aroused Bishop Parker, the State left a heavy financial burden upon the Catholic parents in the performance of this duty.

Bishop Parker was particularly concerned with the developing Catholic Community in Corby and he took the opportunity, when blessing the foundation stone of a new school in Corby in June 1952, to set out his case and concern for Catholic education. Bishop Parker's words on that occasion may serve as a type for the general attitude and policy of the Diocese at the time.

The setting was the great church of Our Lady of Walsingham in Occupation Road, with the long buildings of the Infants' School and Primary School at the rear and at the side, on an ample site, the great steel skeleton of the new Secondary Modern School. A kilted pipe-band led the procession of children and clergy from the church, along the road and then across the future playing fields to the new school to join the large, waiting crowd.

After laying and blessing the foundation stone, Bishop Parker spoke to the parents of the children, recalling how most of them had seen the town of Corby emerge from practically nothing and how they had brought to a new home in England the faith and piety of Catholic homes from far away in Scotland. In the past two years, these Catholics had already expended £30,000 on their church and schools and they were

Bishop Parker blessing the foundation stone of Corby School

now undertaking a further burden of £100,000 or more, in order that their elder children could be educated as Catholics.

He went on to repeat what he had said on an earlier occasion, when opening the old wooden church as an Infants' School. He had hoped that the Butler Education Act of 1944 would have given to Catholic parents the same rights and facilities for education which the Scottish people enjoyed. If the people to whom he was speaking had not come to England to work in the Corby Steel Works and had remained in Scotland, a denominational Catholic School would have been provided for them by the State, without them having to pay a penny; for the education law in Scotland was different from what obtained in England.

Bishop Parker said that if parents in England could not have 'provided schools' to which in conscience they could safely send their children, then England was not a fit place for them to live in. He said that, in the matter of religion, no compromise was possible. There must be the same principles for guiding life, in the home, in the church and in the school. That is why the Catholics of Corby were shouldering a huge financial liability.

The Education Act of 1944 was a disappointment because it gave no relief beyond providing a canteen. He thought that it was a strange anomaly that the working man today must himself pay what were tantamount to fees for his child to attend a school maintained by the Local Education Authority.

To back up his words with spiritual power, Bishop Parker said that he would be joining the children and their parents who would be going, on the following day, to the shrine at Walsingham, 'to tell the Mother of God, the powerful patron of their school, of their needs and our distress'.

In 1965, Bishop Parker was still fighting the battle for Catholic schools when a new problem had arisen. The Diocese was now very much harassed by the new idea at that time of comprehensive schools. In 1936, it had been recommended that the all-age schools, which had been built at much sacrifice, should 'be decapitated of seniors'. In 1944, this had become an order and the Catholics had to build new Senior Secondary Schools. Now, before these had been paid for, there was the new idea of three, or two-tier Comprehensive Schools. Bishop Parker said, 'Does not all this additional expense over so short a time appear (it does to me) as rather a breach of trust. I think we should use the word "apprehensive" rather than "comprehensive"'. It was possibly a sign of a growing ecumenism that Bishop Parker could say that, 'Happily, all the major denominations are agreed' on pressing the Government on the point.

Two Catholic schools for the future

So, Bishop Parker had built churches and schools, but probably the building programme that was at the forefront of his mind was the Cathedral. For many years at the beginning of his episcopate, he had been gaining support for his vision of an extension and partial rebuilding of the Cathedral to make it more worthy of its title and a more fitting place for the worship of God. Exercising fully his talent of raising funds, Bishop Parker managed to make his dream a reality in 1955.

The Second Vatican Council (1962-1965)

In happy and great old age, the retired Bishop Parker woke up after an afternoon nap. Looking a bit startled, he said, 'Sometimes we wonder where we are.' And, in a lower voice, he confided, 'Sometimes we wonder who we are!'

Quite a number of Catholics, including some priests, possibly had a similar experience as

4 - The Council Years (1950-1975)

they became aware of the effects of Vatican II. Like some people at the end of World War II, they were hoping that now life in the Church would return to normal and be as it was before the Council. But, as in the post-war situation, that could not be. Things had changed and would change further. It was now the task of the Bishops to manage that change.

Charles Grant had been made Auxiliary Bishop to Leo Parker in 1961 and so they both attended the Council. It is not known what they expected, but whatever it was, they were doubtless as surprised as the other English Bishops by the outcome. They, too, found it a steep learning experience. Bishop Grant made a speech at the Council about Justice and Peace and particularly about Third World poverty and the immorality of nuclear weapons, thus contributing to the debate that led to the 'Constitution on the Church in the Modern World'.

English Bishops at The Second Vatican Council

The two Bishops quickly realised the way the Council was leading and they kept the Diocese informed of progress. Bishop Parker was to retire in 1967, two years after the close of the Council, and so it fell to Bishop Grant to put the Council's programme into effect in the Diocese.

Bishop Grant at the Commission for Justice and Peace

The first document of the Council to be promulgated was 'The Constitution on the Sacred Liturgy' and it was the reforms of the liturgy that made most immediate impact on the people in the parishes. For some, changes to simplify the structure of the Mass, the greater prominence given to Scripture and the use of the vernacular, were welcome. Indeed some, both laity and clergy, had been promoting these ideas for some time.

Fr McCormack, the Travelling Missioner, wrote in 1965, 'I think a word about the recent changes in the Liturgy of the Church would not be out of place here. The use of English in the Mass and the permission to say Mass facing the people, have been of tremendous help in the work of the Travelling Mission. I have long been convinced that if notable progress is to be made in making the worship of the Church intelligible, both to Catholics and non-Catholics, then English will have to be used. Without an intelligible form of worship, we have no hope of interesting the vast majority of the people. I am not naive enough to think that just because English is used in the Liturgy or worship, great numbers of people will come flocking to the Church immediately, but surely we have an obligation to remove any unnecessary barriers in the way of people coming nearer and into the Church. My work on the Travelling Mission has convinced me that one of the great barriers has been the use of Latin.

'I cannot describe the sense of frustration which often used to come over me when saying Mass at some of the Mission Centres, with the realisation that in some cases none of the people gathered round an altar for Mass had any point of contact whatsoever with the importance of what was going on. The air of unintelligent passivity on the faces of the people, especially the children, made my heart ache. The amazing thing to me was that these people were at Mass at all. The heartache produced a great urge (no doubt an impatient one at times) to ask and pray for permission to use English in the form of worship.

'The fruits of the first two stages of the reform of the worship of the Church are now beginning to make themselves felt. The people, and especially the children, are now realising what it is to be able to join actively with the priest in the worship of God - and now that the altar is facing them they are beginning to have some realisation of the significance of the Last Supper - something to which they are invited by Christ, something which they can see, something in which they can take part.

'I hope these few words will be of help to those who cannot overcome their horror of change within the Church. Such people must try to get rid of the idea that the Church is a cosy club in which they can sit back in their same old chairs and listen to the same old soporific noises. They must come to a realisation that the Church's doors are open to all men and that they must do their utmost to show all men the way inside. Catholic doctrine is the only touchstone of membership. It is up to us all to present Catholic doctrine to all men in a manner which all men can understand.'

These words expressed the attitude of many people. There had already been some changes in the liturgy before the Council. Changes had been made, for example, to the Roman Missal in 1956. The Rite of Mass had been simplified by reducing the number of commemorations - i.e. prayers added to the Collect (opening prayer) and Post Communion. The Calendar and liturgical year had similarly been tidied up. But these were changes in rubrics that really were of concern only to the priests. It is not likely that the people noticed them. The Easter Vigil liturgy had been restored, but to the people this just appeared as an addition of another celebration at Easter and so it was accepted with no objection. The reform of the liturgy effected by Vatican II was of a different order and affected everyone in the Church.

Not everybody welcomed the changes to the Mass. A significant minority saw them as a threat to the Catholic Faith itself and stood out for the retention of the old form of Mass - the Tridentine Rite. It was in the otherwise obscure corner of Norfolk, Downham Market, that this protest against the revised rite of Mass found its champion and focus, in the parish priest, Fr Oswald Baker.

At first, Bishop Grant tolerated Fr Baker's refusal to celebrate Mass in the new rite. When, however, Fr Baker was going to impose the Tridentine Rite on to the congregation of a newly combined parish of Downham Market and Swaffham, Bishop Grant had to act. The affair was now attracting national publicity and there was the threat of a great public demonstration by Fr Baker and his supporters. After a lot of fruitless negotiations, Bishop Grant had to remove Fr Baker as parish priest by legal process. This Downham Market affair caused much concern and pain to Bishop Grant and highlights some of the difficulties that were encountered in trying to put the Council's resolutions into effect.

Generally speaking, however, Bishop Grant managed pretty well in guiding the Diocese through the post-Vatican II years. The liturgy was only the first area of the Church's life to be affected by the Council. Others, such as ecumenism, would follow, but these would be more prominent later. Meanwhile, in 1975, what was occupying the minds of Bishop Grant and the clergy and people of the Diocese, was the proposal that the Diocese should be divided, giving rise to the new Diocese of East Anglia.

5.
Moving Out - Moving On (1976-2000)

❖

Some priests, across the counties in our Eastern Region, on waking up on 14 March 1976, may well have echoed the words of Bishop Parker, 'We wonder where we are'. Practically overnight, they had been moved out of Northampton Diocese and into a new Diocese called East Anglia, without taking a single step.

Divided

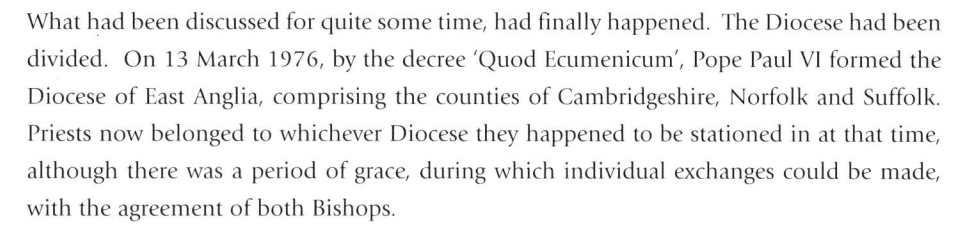

What had been discussed for quite some time, had finally happened. The Diocese had been divided. On 13 March 1976, by the decree 'Quod Ecumenicum', Pope Paul VI formed the Diocese of East Anglia, comprising the counties of Cambridgeshire, Norfolk and Suffolk. Priests now belonged to whichever Diocese they happened to be stationed in at that time, although there was a period of grace, during which individual exchanges could be made, with the agreement of both Bishops.

Charles Grant remained Bishop of Northampton and Alan Clark became Bishop of the new Diocese of East Anglia. He was already a familiar figure there, as he had been Auxiliary Bishop to Bishop Grant since 1969 and had had special responsibility for that eastern part of Northampton Diocese.

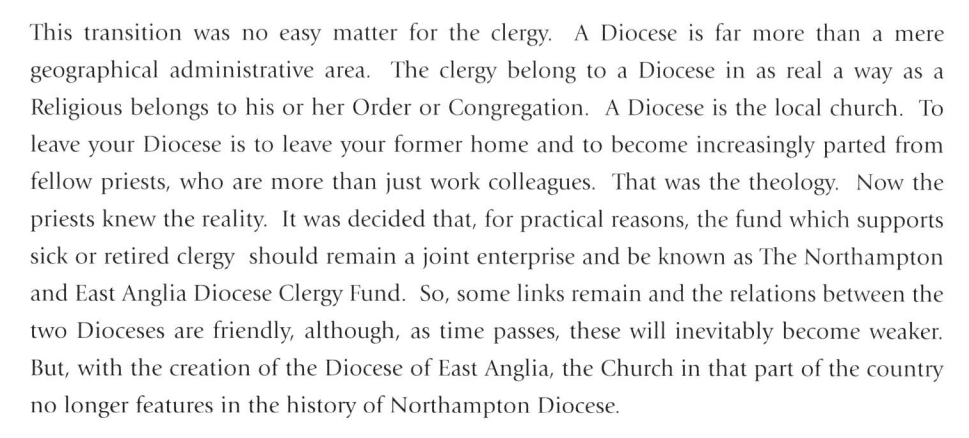

Bishop Clark of East Anglia

This transition was no easy matter for the clergy. A Diocese is far more than a mere geographical administrative area. The clergy belong to a Diocese in as real a way as a Religious belongs to his or her Order or Congregation. A Diocese is the local church. To leave your Diocese is to leave your former home and to become increasingly parted from fellow priests, who are more than just work colleagues. That was the theology. Now the priests knew the reality. It was decided that, for practical reasons, the fund which supports sick or retired clergy should remain a joint enterprise and be known as The Northampton and East Anglia Diocese Clergy Fund. So, some links remain and the relations between the two Dioceses are friendly, although, as time passes, these will inevitably become weaker. But, with the creation of the Diocese of East Anglia, the Church in that part of the country no longer features in the history of Northampton Diocese.

What, then, was Northampton left with? Of course, Walsingham had gone, although it must be noted that, for some years now, it had become a National Shrine and had ceased to be the responsibility of the Bishop of Northampton. And the present Diocese of Northampton still has its well supported annual pilgrimage there. Several priests are known to regret the fact that they no longer have the chance to be appointed to a parish near the sea, although they could always retire there if they wished.

The links with Cambridge were also broken. But, here again, things had already changed in recent years. The University Chaplaincy was under the control of the Catholic Education Board and the Northampton Diocese's involvement with the Chaplaincy had declined in recent years. As for St. Edmund's House, originally a Hall for Secular Clergy, it had later accepted lay students and then non-Catholics. In more recent years, it strove for autonomy within the university, gained College status and elected, as President, a distinguished academic who happened to be an atheist.

Clergy

Of course, with the division, the Catholic population of Northampton Diocese was reduced, as was also the number of priests. It is interesting to compare the figures over the period from 1950 and also to notice the ratio of priests to people.

Date	Catholic Population	Secular Priests	Religious Priests	Total Priests	Ratio
1950	59,143	124	64	188	1 : 315
1955	91,972	124	94	218	1 : 422
1960	123,060	148	102	250	1 : 492
1965	163,144	162	120	282	1 : 579
1970	184,417	174	102	276	1 : 668
1975	196,280	170	108	278	1 : 706
1980	141,669	115	64	179	1 : 791
1985	147,864	119	54	173	1 : 855
1990	159,596	108	58	166	1 : 961
1995	172,484	103	35	138	1 : 1250

When Bishop Wareing reported to Rome, in 1854, that the Diocese has 30 priests, he noted that they were 'all natives' — that is, either all from the Diocese, or all English. Such is not the case today. Some few years back, the Diocese, in common with many other English Dioceses, received a substantial influx of priests from Ireland and the Diocese is very grateful for their work here. Several of these remain with the Diocese today, but that source of priests has now almost dried up. Certainly, some candidates are coming from Irish families, but these are families that have settled here some time ago. The Diocese, however, has received priests, or candidates from other parts of England and from abroad. There are priests from Poland and Malta and a seminarian who is from Vietnam.

As is clear from the figures quoted above, the Diocese has for many years relied on a significant number of priests who are members of Religious Orders. Some Orders have staffed certain parishes, often for many years. In addition, there are several priests who were Religious, but have subsequently been incardinated into the Diocese. The Italians have their own church and priests at St. Frances Cabrini in Bedford and the Poles have their church and priests in Northampton.

In 1997 and early 1998, five priests were ordained who had previously been priests in the Church of England and who had left to become Catholics in the wake of the Church of England's ordination of women. What was particularly new about this was that two of these priests are married men with families. Another such former Anglican priest, who is married, was ordained more recently.

The Diocese took advantage of the restoration of the Permanent Diaconate following Vatican II and took something of a lead in ordaining men, including married men, to the Diaconate. There are, at present, about twenty such deacons and several more are expected to be ordained in the next few years. The people in the parishes have welcomed both the deacons and the married priests and value their ministry.

Bishop Thomas with Permanent Deacons

Ecumenism

Another area where Northampton Diocese has been leading in recent years is ecumenism. The Diocese followed the lead given by Vatican II and developed friendly relations with other Christians. Then, there was involvement ecumenically in various places in shared projects and activities. A Diocesan Ecumenical Commission was set up fairly early on and there is a Diocesan Ecumenical Officer. In the early nineteen-eighties, the Benedictine monks and nuns came from Cockfosters to Turvey to set up the Monastery of Christ Our Saviour and the Priory of Our Lady of Peace. They are devoted, in a special way, to the cause of Christian Unity and contribute strongly to the work of ecumenism.

Benedictines at Turvey

A significant step forward was the establishment of shared churches. Probably the first of these was at Cippenham. There is another at Downley, High Wycombe and one at Wendover. The most obviously ecumenical scene is in the new 'city' of Milton Keynes. Starting in the nineteen-seventies, Milton Keynes was a completely new settlement, that has become famous as the site of the Open University and many centres of technology. The Diocese obviously had to make provision for the very many Catholics among those who were settling there. Most of the Christian Churches there were committed to ecumenism from the start and the City wanted all new churches to be shared.

Cippenam

Downley, December 1975

Bishop Grant, however, thought that, with people arriving in a disoriented state, the first priority must be an identifiable Catholic Church. When several parishes were well established, the policy changed under Bishop Thomas. Now Christ the King is a shared church and part of the Walton ecumenical project. The Catholic Church at Coffee Hall also serves the Ecumenical Church of Christ the Cornerstone.

In 1987, the then Archbishop of Canterbury, Robert Runcie, visited Milton Keynes and came to an ecumenical service at St. Augustine's, with the theme, 'Not Strangers, but Pilgrims'. The Anglican Bishops of Oxford and Buckingham and the leaders of the Methodist and United Reformed churches were present with Bishop Francis Thomas of Northampton. The Baptist Superintendent presided.

A Catholic priest took a regular turn with other local ministers in leading Sunday services for an ecumenical congregation at Hodge Lea. There has been an occasional shared Eucharist, with an Anglican and a Catholic priest presiding at neighbouring altars.

Commissioning of Rev. Hugh Cross, Ecumenical Moderator of Milton Keynes, April 1991

Bishop Thomas signed the constitution of the local ecumenical project in the Wavendon area and he also took a full part in the presidency of the Milton Keynes Christian Council, meeting with other church leaders to develop the policies for the church life in Milton Keynes. In common with other presidents, Bishop Thomas was a trustee of the financial appeal for the projected City Centre Church.

Two Religious Sisters also played a full part in the ecumenical work in the late eighties, being financed partly by the Anglican Diocese of Oxford and partly by their Religious Orders. One Sister was a member, and later the leader, of an Ecumenical Team, while another became a City Centre Chaplain, in 1987, and a member of the Team Ministry.

Working together

All this is rather different from the attitude of the Catholics in the Diocese at an earlier time. Then, the talk and action was of refuting the Protestants, establishing Catholic missions and promoting such Associations as The Guild of St. Felix and St. Edmund, which was formed in 1930 with the aim of 'forwarding the work of reconverting East Anglia to the Ancient Faith'. Things have moved on, but they have not become any simpler. Of course, the Catholics of the Diocese follow the lead given by Pope John Paul II and the late Cardinal Hume. They know that the Church is committed to ecumenism and that we are to move from co-operation to commitment, but for some, it does make their awareness of their Catholic identity less clear. They possibly, like the awakened Bishop Parker, 'sometimes wonder who we are'.

Dennis Taylor opening the Life office, Northampton

The Laity

Over the years, the focus of the laity has changed in other ways. Whereas, in an earlier period, they were more concerned with matters within the Church, now, it could be argued, they are having their attention drawn to the world outside. This is in line with the teaching about the role and mission of the laity - as in 'Christifideles Laici'.

This shift can be seen to some extent by comparing the contents of the Diocesan Directories of, say, the nineteen-fifties with more recent ones. Apart from the factual information about Mass times and the like, the early Directories contain articles on matters that the Bishop and editor considered the laity needed to be instructed in. So, in the Directories for several years in the nineteen-fifties, we read about what to do when the priest makes a Sick Call (2 pages). There is an extensive treatment on the regulations, both Church and civil, concerning marriage. Seven closely printed pages set out 'Catholic Faith and Practice' by Fr Alphonsus Bonnar O.F.M. This is really a condensed form of manual-type Theology. Then, there is a full page on 'The Order of kneeling, standing and sitting at Sung High Mass', containing twenty-three separate directives. In some years, the Directories give details about the laws of fasting and abstinence, the changes in the Roman Missal, the prohibition of Catholic children attending non-Catholic schools and, finally, an article on Indulgences.

If we turn to more recent Directories, these topics are absent. Instead, more attention is given to what might be called Christian Social Matters. In 1987, there is an article about the Northampton Diocesan Pastoral Service for the Deaf and Hard of Hearing, whose aim is to enable hearing impaired people to share fully in the life of the Christian Community. It is

Luton Day Centre for the homeless

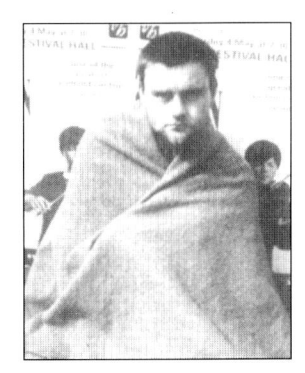

reported that a conference on Catholic Social Teaching took place in 1993, as a follow-up to the National Centenary of 'Rerum Novarum'.

In 1997, there was an account of the Luton Day Centre for the Homeless. What began with a small group of S.V.P. members seeking ways to help needy Irish people, who were calling at presbyteries, grew into a substantial organisation, providing care at a Day Centre. The services, providing meals, medical care and training, were opened to needy people of all sorts. As the project grew, the organisers joined with other churches and also gained the co-operation of the Borough Council. In the same Directory, there is an account of the work of a group from Burnham and Slough, who help people living on the streets in London, offering them food, friendship, clothing, bedding and, when asked, referral to social agencies.

In the 1999 Directory, fifty-six societies and organisations, that are respresented in the Northampton Diocese, are listed. They range from what may be termed spiritual groups, such as the Association of Our Lady of Mount Carmel, Catholic Charismatic Renewal and Christian Life Community; through more social action groups, such as CAFOD, Life and Beginning Experience; to more specialised associations, like the Association of Catholic Women, The English Catholic History Association and the Guild of St. Agatha for bellringers.

A notable development in recent years has been that of lay ministries, of which Readers and Eucharistic Ministers are, possibly, the most obvious, but there are many more. Although not many new schools have been built in this period, Religious Education has not lacked attention. The emphasis has been on training Catechists and, even, Key Catechists for work in the parishes.

The Assembly

Many initiatives involving the laity arose from, or were strengthened by, the Diocesan Assembly. The Assembly, strictly speaking, was a weekend event in May 1988, that took place at St. Thomas Becket School, Northampton. But to say just that, would be to give an entirely inadequate picture.

Bishop Thomas explained that it was 'a process in which the life and mission of the Diocese were coming under review and in which the priests and people were being called together to share their experiences and their hopes'. There were two years of preparation. The clergy were taken out of their parishes for a week's study on two occasions. In the preparation period, there were meetings in parishes and at Deanery and Diocesan level and delegates were selected. The process was co-ordinated by Fr Paul Hardy and a steering committee, and it was led, or facilitated, by a group from the Movement for a Better World.

Bishop Thomas attends The Assembly, 1988

The Assembly, 1988

Diocesan Steering Group for Marriage and Family Life

Then came the Assembly weekend. There were workshops on a variety of aspects of the Church's life in the Diocese and the groups were to present reports and resolutions for future action. The whole process came to a climax in the final Eucharist and the presentation of the resolutions. In 1990, a report was issued, detailing some of the outcome of the Assembly. There was mention of a Council of Religious and a programme of Vocations Promotion. The Diocesan Communications Team had created a network of Deanery Communications Officers and parish contacts. The Adult Education Service had made progress and the areas of evangelisation and spirituality were receiving attention. In 1989, a Diocesan Steering Group for Marriage and Family Life had started their work of encouraging existing groups in the Diocese. There was talk of a Master Plan for the Diocese. The Diocesan Youth Service got a boost from the Assembly and Diocesan, Deanery and Parish pastoral councils were established.

Whatever else may be said, there has certainly been a proliferation of groups and meetings, but that is possibly the Church reflecting a trend in contemporary society. How fruitful it will be for spreading the Kingdom is questioned by some and remains to be seen.

Outlook

The Diocese seems to be not unlike the Church in general, in that it is now looking more beyond its own confines. So, we have some Diocesan priests as Chaplains to the Forces and others have served in Peru with the Society of St. James. Several priests, with Religious and laity, minister as chaplains in state prisons, NHS hospitals and secular universities and colleges.

There are some negative signs, which are common to all Dioceses in England. The percentage of the Catholic population who regularly attend Mass has fallen and there is some concern about the smaller number of men offering themselves for ordination to the priesthood.

Obviously, these matters need close attention and, as the Diocese moves into the next century, a priority for it must be the evangelisation not only of the secular society, but also of its own baptised, but somewhat dormant, members. This would seem to require not just some more schemes, or systems, or projects, but a deeper appreciation of current theology.

When Bishop Leo McCartie retires in September 2000, the Diocese will, of course, need a new Bishop. Perhaps, however, there is truth in Newman's comment that the Church, at the time, had more need of theologians than it had of Bishops. The ideal, of course, is to have both, but that is for the future.

After the division of the Diocese in 1976, Northampton Diocese was cut off from the sea that had formerly lapped its Eastern border. But it has not been cut off from the 'Sea of Faith'. The history of the past hundred and fifty years of Northampton Diocese has been the story of the returning tide of that Sea of Faith. Has that tide now reached it height? Is it now beginning to ebb, as some think, or is it still flowing strongly, but being led into different channels? Only history can tell.